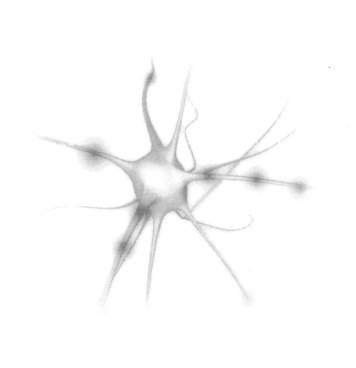

A NEW BRAIN
FOR BUSINESS

Richard S. Trafton, Ph.D.
and
S. Diane Marentette

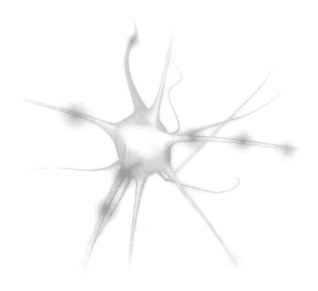

ISBN: 978-0-615-35748-5

Published by
The New Brain for Business Institute

www.newbrainforbusiness.com

Table of Contents

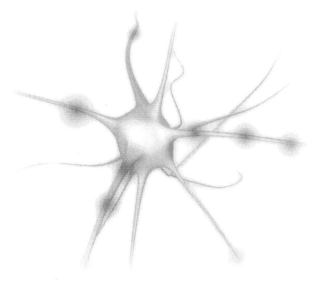

Introduction

Over the years, we have had the privilege to work with so many smart, capable people across a wide range of businesses, large and small. Often, after an intense session, a client would ask, "Where can I read more about this stuff?" Because our work is based on such a wide range of ideas and concepts in both science and business, we could point to no single place that offered a practical, integrated point of view on leadership that aligned with the work we do.

So, this book is for our clients, first and foremost, because you asked!

We also set out to write this book because we see so many organizations underperforming. This is not to say that they are failing, or even failing to make money. Rather, we see how great an organization can be if great leadership allows everyone to do and be their best.

Ask yourself this question: In your organization, is everyone doing the very best they can, every day? Are you really getting all that your people have to offer? We have yet to come across an organization where the answer to that question is "yes."

Our experience and pursuit of understanding how to achieve the best from ourselves and others gives us a hint at the immense potential in the human endeavor. Yet, so often we fail to realize it. We can imagine organizations becoming so effective that they redefine the meaning of business success. The markers of success in business, such as EBIT, ROI, share price, etc., would have to be re-calibrated if people were really doing their best, all the time. This is one goal of the New Brain For Business.

We also believe that when an organization does become so effective and successful in this way, the individuals in the company will reap enormous benefits as well. Not just in terms of money, but in terms of a sense of well being. When people are engaged in great work, their hearts and minds grow commensurately. So, this book is for anyone who feels they can get more from themselves and their people and are looking for ideas about how to do so.

Over the years, we have built upon ideas from many areas of study, including psychology, evolutionary biology, neurology, economics, business, and sociology. Theories that have informed our consulting practice range from the broad, such as Darwin's work on evolution, to the very specific, like the field studies of brood size in blackbirds! Since we are talking about leadership in business, this book isn't about any of these theories in particular. Rather, it draws upon them all in an attempt to explain why we do what we do in the workplace.

We have an intense interest in the circumstances in which people are at their best.

- Where do people do their best work?
- What conditions allow people to be their most creative?
- When do we see people offering their best thinking and problem solving?
- When do people communicate most effectively?

This is the critical question that guides our approach: where do people achieve their best? That is, where do people feel complete, whole, and integrated? Where do they feel that they are doing something of value, that truly matters? Where do they feel they, themselves, are of value? What drives us is the pursuit of this: we want you to *do* your best and *be* your best.

This of course translates directly to leadership. Leadership is where you help others do their best and be their best. Simultaneous success in both these endeavors is no mean feat. Being your best and doing your best yourself is the first step in being a great leader. Great leadership doesn't require perfection, but it does benefit from humility and commitment to being and doing *your* best.

What is going on in this human machine of ours as we attempt to create successful businesses? Wherever we go, we bring our complete human selves with us. Every bit of who we are is with us at all times, no matter the circumstances. By understanding some of the basics of how we operate because of our "human being-ness," we can make better choices - choices that help us do our best and be our best.

Here is an important note: doing your best and being your best does not mean being at your peak at all times. There is a natural ebb and flow of our energy, attention, and intention across each day. Some days you do better thinking than on other days. Some days you are a better listener than on other days. Doing your best means being the best you can be in any given moment, even if you know you have done better on other days.

Similarly, being your best varies from day to day and from time to time. One cannot be upbeat and enthusiastic all the time. Being your best means getting the most out of a particular moment, even if other moments felt a lot better.

Most of us operate under a myth in business (and often in life in general). We think of it as the 110% rule. There is this unfortunate and unrealistic belief on the part of many leaders that they and their people can and should show up and operate at "110%" every day.

This is an example of the kind of misinformation we attack in this book. We don't dwell on popular opinion. Instead, we recommend leader behaviors be built on sound science. So, for example, we dismiss the notion of "stretch goals." They are just another way to help people feel like failures. We offer alternative thinking based on solid research about setting goals and enabling success.

Leadership isn't just about the science, of course. We combine it with our decades of consulting, teaching, and coaching experience, as well as our years as leaders ourselves in various roles. Every single suggestion offered in this book has been tried by us and our clients. We know this stuff works!

How To Read This Book

We have condensed a lot of theory, thinking, and practice into a format intended to be friendly to any leader who wants to immediately increase his or her effectiveness. You can take a deep dive or you can pick a few nuggets out and move on. And there is plenty of space in between these two extremes. Each chapter stands on its own, if you like.

Each chapter beginning with Chapter 4 is organized in this way:

- It presents an overview of a leadership issue that occurs daily in business.

- We follow this with real stories about real leaders in real organizations facing this issue. We have, of course, changed the names and been vague about the organization, because knowing these details is not important to your getting something out of these stories. Each of these stories could be set in another industry and the message would be the same.

- Then we present a brief dip into the science behind this particular issue.

- We close each chapter with a series of behaviors and tools you can use to be more effective in this particular situation. Sometimes the same exercise or action is suggested in more than one chapter. This is intentional and reflects two objectives.

  - To insure that each chapter can be read on its own without reference to other chapters.

  - Some of these tools are more powerful than others and have broader application. The more often you see something in this book, the more powerful we think it is. If something looks familiar, don't skip it! Each presentation will have a slightly different spin to fit the situation. These differences can add to your understanding.

If you are in a hurry and just want to address a specific leadership challenge in your organization, just browse the Table of Contents, find your area of interest and go to that chapter. Then go directly to the "What Can You Do" section and read the behavioral suggestions. You can put them to work right away. It is not necessary to understand why these things work. *They just do*. They work even if you don't read the stories that showcase the issue, or if you skip the scientific summary explaining why. We think you will be more effective if you do read the rest, but you can improve your effectiveness as a leader by *engaging in the behavior*. Period.

If your goal is a better understanding of what makes up great leadership, read Chapters 1 through 4 first. The background here on brain science and evolution can be helpful in shaping your thinking about leadership.

Once you have this foundation, you can move through the remaining chapters in any order you choose, with the exception of the final chapter, Moving Forward. We have tried to sequence the chapters with a certain sense of flow, but you can alter the order without major consequence.

To Our Clients

Each leader and each situation presented in this book is, in a sense, a real person in a real organization. Because of our respect for our clients, we have altered some of the information to insure anonymity. If you think you see yourself, you are probably right, but not because we are writing about you! If you recognize yourself, assume that we had more than one leader in mind when we chose the issue and wrote the story. Understand that if it is hitting close to home, it is because you have struggled with this issue!

In any case, we have worked hard to insure realistic representation of leadership in action without putting anyone in an uncomfortable position.

This book is possible because of our clients. The trust they have placed in us over the years is both humbling and deeply rewarding. Their willingness to share parts of themselves and to teach us is a gift beyond price. We hope that the value they find here serves as some small repayment of their gift.

Rich Trafton and Diane Marentette

I.
Making a Case for Seeing Leadership Differently

Despite a plethora of leadership theories, books and training over the past 30 or more years, there is no easy answer to leading people toward great business results. Having learned the "Five Steps to. . ." or "21 Ways..." in leadership, we still find ourselves in the worst economic downturn in over a half-century.

There are many explanations for how we got where we are - with failing banks, stock market free-fall, and joblessness at a frightening level. There are, however, no easy answers to a turnaround, just as there are no easy answers to being successfully, happily, peacefully human.

Under such dire business circumstances, how does a leader find within him or herself the best behavior, the best thinking, the best reactions and therefore the best *leadership* to help those within the organization find those same "bests" within themselves? How do we help others do their very best work and be their very best person?

The fact is that during our lifetimes, we face major changes regularly. We are challenged to learn from them and move on, and ultimately we either make changes within ourselves to find our "bests," or we do not. If we don't, typically there is an ending less satisfying than we hoped.

The fact that the world continually changes around us and we live through these major changes does not mean we ourselves change easily. In fact, the opposite is true: personal change is typically *slow, incremental* and *painful.* In fact, if it is *not* all three of these, we may just be fooling ourselves into thinking we are changing.

Personal change is slow, incremental and painful. If it is not all three, you are fooling yourself into thinking you are changing.

Here, we will not address all the possible explanations about how we got into this very messy business situation that surrounds us (such as banking failures, foreclosures, the recession, and the like), but we will address leadership issues that we think make a large contribution to the problems we as a society face.

Let us begin by understanding more about what is true about being human and what that implies about leading other humans to some successful future place.

On Being Human: Our Brains Make the Difference

Have you thought much about how our brains evolved? Through thorough study and scientific research, we know that humans did not start out the way we are now, with the ability to ponder complex issues or produce sophisticated engineering and art forms. In fact, we are now at a point in our evolution where we can look back and see where we came from, and we also can imagine our future to a degree. Let us begin with a look back, to find the cherished nuggets – the roots – of leadership in our past.

You have read books or seen documentaries about very early humans in their quite primitive environment, so imagine what you believe to be true about it.

The drivers of behavior were relatively simple. Most of the day was spent pursuing, collecting and consuming food. There was no language (although there were forms of communication). Tools, if any, were primitive, such as sticks or rocks. Now, further imagine one of these humans. Let's call him Gur, though it is not likely he actually had a name. Gur is walking down a crude path in this landscape, his task being to collect fruits, berries, or other edibles for his clan and himself to eat.

Along this particular path there is a fig tree just a bit off the trail. This tree is laden with ripe fruit. The clan can eat well on the fruit of this tree! The clan is counting on Gur to bring back some food. Unfortunately, Gur walks past the fig tree and does not see it is ripe with fruit. He has missed an opportunity to feed himself and the clan.

Hopefully, others are out finding and gathering food as well, but these figs could be all the food the clan was going to get that day, and they will now go to sleep hungry. Both Gur and the clan, however, will likely recover and have an opportunity to look for and find food tomorrow. If this pattern of overlooking food persists, of course, then the clan is likely to be in trouble. But the trouble, if it exists, is some way off and there are opportunities for recovery.

Now imagine that walking down this same path, Gur hears a rustle in the bushes. There is no certainty about the cause: it could be a small rodent, a bird, or a deadly predator. In Gur's world, if he does not hear the rustle or if he does not respond rapidly and effectively upon hearing it, the risk of *death* is significant. Perhaps it was responding to this rustle that kept Gur from noticing the figs!

The truth of Gur's circumstances is this: if he fails to notice, orient and respond quickly to this potential threat, he is less likely to contribute to the gene pool in the future.

A key evolutionary lesson:
Missed opportunity is much less costly
than missed threat.

Compared to the missed figs, this is a much more critical error. Here is the key evolutionary lesson: in general, *missed opportunity* is much less costly than *missed threat*.

Over evolutionary time, our brain structures have developed to reflect this important difference. So, our brains are very potent in the realm of attending and responding to risk or threat, and much less potent in attending and responding to opportunities.

Consider the "life-dinner" principle. Why does the rabbit run faster than the fox? Quite simply, the fox is running for his dinner and the rabbit is running for his life. You decide which is the more potent motivator.

Adaptation in the human realm has been similar,

and just as formidable, dominant and well sustained. Think about this: Gur did not stop to ponder the rustle, nor did he say to himself, "Guess the figs will have to wait." Gur survived to find the figs another day because of behavior that was automatic, immediate, and critical to survival. If he did not, it would not be Gur who kept the clan going over time. Those who were able to quickly assess and attend to risk survived to pass on their genetic package, so that future clan members would be as or more likely to survive.

In large part, the brain being developed in Gur's era is the foundational structure for the brain we have today. Let's look at our brain from a structural perspective. There are three parts to the brain that we will discuss in the hopes that it is helpful to understanding the similarities and differences between humans today and Gur and his clan. What follows describes a bit about the structure and function of each section and what each portends for the challenges leaders face today.

Old Brain, New Brain

It is helpful to think of the brain as having three layers, from "top" to "bottom," if you will. Although we will lump the bottom two layers, they are actually different and so we describe each separately.

Brain Stem. This area of the brain controls very fundamental metabolic functions like blood pressure, body temperature, and organ functioning. It also has the power to preclude higher-order functions if there is imminent danger to these metabolic functions. This is why if your heart begins to beat in a dangerous way, you may pass out – the brain stem basically shuts the rest of the brain down to attend to the physical body condition.

Mid-Brain or "Old" Brain. This is the home for emotions. Many people imagine that our emotions exist in our hearts, because we can *feel* an ache there when we are emotionally hurt.   In fact, we feel emotions in many parts of our body ("jitters," "butterflies in the stomach") but emotions are initially processed in this part of the brain.

While the mid-brain does not have the priority to take precedence over the brain stem, it certainly interacts with and influences it.

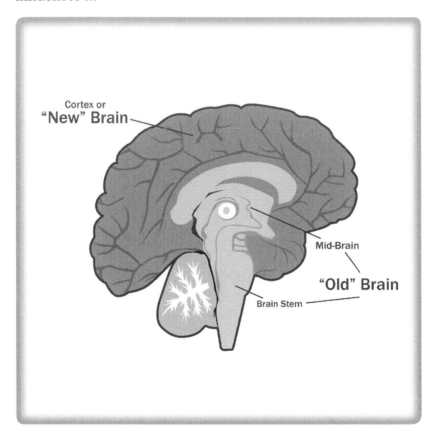

We all have experienced being startled and know that this can cause increased pulse rates, pupil dilation, and a release of chemicals that readies our muscles for action.   These physical responses, while fundamentally driven by the brain stem, are clearly initiated by the emotional part of our brain.

The mid-brain is also a filter for all incoming perceptual information.   That is right, *all* of our perceptions are filtered first through our emotional brain before we ever have an opportunity to *think* about them.   This is the part of the brain that Gur was helping us develop: rustle in the bushes, mid-brain processing of the threat, *RUN!*

Based on scientific research, we now know that about **90%** of the physical wiring in the mid-brain is associated with one single emotion: fear. This processing of emotion or filtering of our perceptions developed as protection for us – is there something dangerous or threatening here?   It is hard not to appreciate that early contribution.

All perceptual information gets filtered by your old brain before anything else happens.

Humans are incredibly adept at processing and responding to threat or danger. Think about this: although it is measured in milli-seconds and therefore not obvious to us, we actually take *twice as long* to completely process a "danger" word (thief) than a "safe" word (friend) What is happening during this additional time? Your old brain is filtering for danger. If danger is detected, your old brain will begin defensive activity, without your awareness.   When we filter and discover a threat, we can act before we have had any time to think.   Have you ever jumped back when startled?   Of course!   Those who did not were "culled" from the breeding stock long ago.

The mid-brain cannot control the brain stem (we can wish to lower our body temperature when we are too hot, but we cannot do it by just having a strong emotional reaction to the heat). The mid-brain *is* powerful enough to take precedence over higher levels in the brain, which we'll describe more fully shortly.

Taken together, the brain stem and the mid-brain comprise what many call the "old" brain, because it is old in an evolutionary sense. The old brain is exquisitely attuned to noticing, orienting and responding to "rustles in the bushes." The old brain is truly our protector, and we can honor and respect the protection it provides us. That prickle on the back of your neck as you walk out into a dark parking lot late at night is your old brain looking out for you.

The old brain is the brain contained in Gur's skull. Although there has undoubtedly been some evolution of the old brain since Gur's time, the fact is that there is not that much difference between Gur's brain and our "old" brain today. This is not about brain size, but rather about the differentiation in structure that has taken place over hundreds of thousands, if not millions, of years.

Our fundamental survival is foremost even now. Evolution has given us an extremely effective system for detecting and responding to threat or danger that is still very active. We have hints about it daily. Imagine you are stuck in a traffic jam because there is an accident on the other side of the road. Our old brains won't just let us drive by without checking out the risk associated with the situation. This is beyond morbid curiosity.

This is primal adaptation in action. Even though we logically know that we are not in the accident, and that it won't involve us, we have to look anyway. This may give you a hint as to why "bad news sells."

There is plenty more we can say about the "old" brain, and we will. First let's complete the picture.

Cortex or "New" Brain. The cortex is the residence of what we tend to think of as higher-order brain functions, like language, planning, thinking, analysis, comparison, fine differentiation of detail and the like. Because this portion of the brain evolved more recently, many refer to it as the "new" brain.

While functionally this is an amazing and powerful part of our brain, it can be interrupted, literally in less than a heartbeat, by the old brain. It can do very cool things, but it's not the big dog. In fact, much of the activity in this part of the brain is often applied at the behest of the old brain, which can get us into trouble.

What this means in practical terms is that if there is a "rustle in the bushes" in our current environment, the old brain is likely to be in charge and the amazing higher order functions of the new brain will be put on hold, or at least constrained and sub-optimized.

Our Integrated Brain

While it is true that the brain is one integrated organ, there is a lot of distinct, localized functioning within it. There are innumerable connections called neural pathways between the old brain and the new brain. However, not all pathways are created equal. In fact, the pathways that lead *from* the old brain *to* the new brain are an order of magnitude larger than the pathways that run in the opposite direction. What does this mean in practical terms? It means that our emotions often intrude on our thinking, but our thinking rarely intrudes on our emotions.

Our emotions often intrude
on our thinking,
but our thinking rarely intrudes
on our emotions.

The hierarchy of control is clear and very difficult, some might even say impossible, to override. If we are looking to be and do our best, this is a key point. The best inventions of humanity happened not while sprinting down a path with a predator on our heels, but rather sitting around the clan fire with enough food to go around.

We challenge the notion that necessity is the mother of invention. Rather, necessity leads us to want something. If we want it badly, our old brain will interfere with our getting it. It is our new brain that does the inventing. This can happen only when the old brain is calmed.

Much old brain activity occurs without our being aware of it. The old brain, it seems, is under no obligation to offer up any sort of clear signal to the new brain that it is now taking charge. When someone says to us, "Calm down, you're losing your cool," and we respond stridently, "I most certainly am not," we have an early hint of our old brain taking the reins.

Much of our success as leaders depends upon our ability to recognize and respond positively to these early indicators, and to resist the powerful pull of old brain leadership. And it can be successfully resisted!

As we think back to our intrepid hunter-gatherer walking in the wild, it is easy to see that Gur's energy was directed by old brain processes. As soon as there was a rustle in the bushes, the search for food came to a halt. This is not a decision he made; it was a non-conscious, automatic response. To really understand the power of this message, it helps to take a much closer look at the differences between old brain and new brain behaviors and what they look like in a contemporary work environment.

Managing the balance between our old and new brain is no small feat. The numerous ways our old brain intrudes and takes control, often in ways detrimental to us and our businesses, are so commonplace that they often feel "normal" to us. Starting in

Chapter 4, we will take a deeper dive into some of these old brain characteristics. We will explore situations where real leaders in real companies struggle to do their best work and be their best person.

Let us go next, though, to a look at the new brain in more detail. Then we will follow that with some other brain processes that have a significant impact on the way we lead and run our businesses.

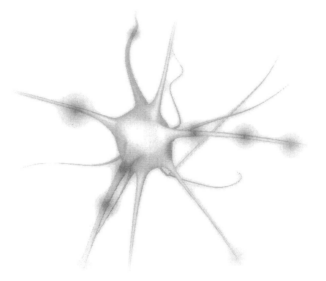

.

2.
Having a New Brain for Business

~~~~~

For an in-depth look at the new brain and its amazing capacities, let's first consider this: In today's business world, what is it that we want most from ourselves, our people, and our organization?

As you think through your personal list, think about what you already know about the old brain. We find that the things we most often seek in business are not forthcoming from the old brain. We will find that passion is an exception here, although this is also a risky tool to use and takes great skill to wield effectively.

More about all the old brain characteristics in later chapters. If what we want is not found in the old brain, it must reside in the new brain. As we go through these characteristics, compare them to your list of what you want from yourself and others in your organization. Let's look at some of these new brain characteristics.

The New Brain is Logical and Analytical

The new brain is a logical, analytical machine. It excels at computation, clever problem solving, and brilliant analysis. Our capacity in this realm is quite astounding. No other organism on the planet comes close to the breadth and depth of our analytic abilities.

Unless we are disabled in some way, we are able to add and subtract within our very first years of schooling. Some of us even have both the interest and capacity to calculate complicated formulae to determine how to accomplish such amazing feats as flying to and landing on the moon!

For perspective, consider the problem solving ability of the next most capable non-human (for example, the chimpanzee). At best, it has the analytical ability of a child approximately two to three years old. No addition or subtraction is happening here, regardless of effort and training. Even when taught a basic version of sign language, the chimp cannot compute, or execute a complex logical task.

It is these thinking skills that have helped us develop the very advanced society we live in today. Everywhere you look you see the fruits of our analytical thinking. The fact that you can read and make some sense of a book is testament to the logical, analytical ability of your new brain.

Humans are the only organisms capable of not only using tools, but also figuring out how to make them better. Consider percussion flaking. This is a technique for banging rocks together to create sharp-edged tools. Many primitive arrowhead artifacts you may have seen were created this way. Long before we were the evolved beings we are today, when we were still living in very humble and simple circumstances, humans would bang rocks together, examine the output and create techniques to make arrowheads, spear points and other stone tools!

Consider how the analytical and logical power of the human brain added great value to the survival and lifestyle of the individual as well as the overall evolution of the clan. This thinking capability was clearly a powerful force. Today, our businesses benefit when we tap into and maximize this ability for logical analysis.

Again, let's compare the closest non-human ability.   A frequently cited example of non-human ingenuity is the use of sticks by chimpanzees in the wild to insert into anthills and extract ants, which are then eaten. Let's give the chimps their due. This is a good adaptation that allows them access to food that would otherwise be unavailable. Very few other examples of using tools are available in nature.

However, there has never been a recorded instance of a chimpanzee watching one of his or her colleagues using this technique and then improving on it. All chimps in the troop use the tool in exactly the same way. Another troop of chimps elsewhere may have found a different way of using a tool for accessing food, but this troop will not use it unless one of those chimps visits and demonstrates.   The learning is always by means of imitation, not on-going adjustment and adaptation. In other words, no analysis is at play here.

In the workplace, we humans use these capabilities in myriad ways to solve the many business problems we regularly face. Business as we know it would simply not be possible if we were unable to analyze a financial statement or were incapable of resolving a manufacturing challenge.

As a leader, it is often the maximum application of this capability that we strive for in ourselves as well as in those who work around us. Using our logical and analytical new brain represents some of the best we have to offer.

The New Brain is Future-Enabled

With some minor exceptions, there are no other living organisms that have the ability to imagine a future. The exceptions are with higher-order primates (principally chimps and bonobos) and some cetaceans (e.g., dolphins) where there is some evidence of anticipation of very near-term future situations.

It is within the functioning of the new brain that we are able to put together stories that paint a picture of a future – both short- and long-term. Here is where we are able to think through alternatives, choose likely scenarios, and make a plan of action that will help ensure we do actually have the future we want. In fact, we apply the powerful thinking just mentioned above to help us choose this future.

As nascent humans began, through random mutations, to manifest some of this forward-thinking capability, clear survival and repro-ductive advantage emerged. Imagine the advantage conferred upon the first humans to be able to *forecast*, at least in a general way, seasonal movement of game animals, or the emergence of fruits at a particular point in time. Building or seeking shelter before seasonal weather shifts surely would have provided some reproductive advantage. Anticipating weather changes based upon specific signs and planning for plant growth completely modified the human life structure from movement to settlement.

In the workplace, we often think those who can best envision a picture of the future of the business or the marketplace are the most capable or valuable.   Setting goals - for ourselves, for others, and for our businesses - is an important manifestation of this looking into the future. We will see later that the creation of a compelling story about the future is often a key leadership challenge.

The New Brain is Language-Enabled

Gur and his clan communicated with some sounds, but mostly body language, gesturing, and facial expressions.   We can see examples of this primitive communication when we observe troops of chimps together. This is because the language capability of the new brain has not yet developed for them.   In fact, the physical structures within the brain that support and enable language did not yet exist. As these structures developed, humans were then able to label things, places, activities, and people in their environment.

Using these labels, it then became possible to accelerate learning of tool use, for example, by moving beyond mere imitation (no small feat in its own right) to instruction and explanation. Imagine the advantages for the clan that first developed these abilities.

Today we are able to form eloquent, complex ideas in the form of language so that others can understand us.   Not only does language help us manage and manipulate our own concepts and ideas, it also helps us share them with others. So, we can share our powerful thinking and problem solving, along with our view of the future and the specific steps necessary to get there. Those adept along these lines are highly esteemed in most business settings.

Of course, we all have different ways of expressing ourselves, so communication continues to be a key challenge in every aspect of our lives. Our old brain has a tendency to inject emotional harmonics into our communications. In fact, it is nearly impossible for this not to be the case, Mr. Spock and other Vulcans being the exception. The important point to note here is that these important capabilities, some of the very best we bring to the table, reside in the new brain exclusively.

The New Brain is Realistic

When our new brain is in the driver's seat, we are better able to see what is real and what is not.   Our strong analytical capabilities assist us here. In the new brain, we process (but not perceive) the input from our senses (sight, hearing, and so forth). We create the world around us from these various inputs. Our excellent thinking machine helps us do this in a way that allows us to get what we want and need from the world.

Young Woman or Old?

One of the ways this happens is through reality testing. The relatively continuous thinking, analysis, and experimentation we engage in are the foundation for our sense of reality.   We create and test hypotheses about the world around us to achieve what we want. This is a far cry from the crude approximation of reality that exists in our old brain, which will be further investigated throughout this book.

A key differentiator in business is the ability to accurately perceive and understand the marketplace. Leaders who can do this (and share it effectively with others) tend to run more successful businesses. While we use a variety of tools to accomplish this, the seat of this activity is the new brain, yours and that of the people around you.

The New Brain Is Creative

When it comes to thinking outside the box, the new brain excels. Not only can we use our new brain to look into the future, we can use it to look to solutions or adventures that haven't occurred before. We can imagine microprocessors and penicillin.

The adaptive value of creativity can't be overstated. Early humans were eventually able to move beyond imitation to the point of "that was good, but what about if we try this as well?" Instead of just doing what others do, we can imagine doing more or doing it differently. The seat of this kind of thinking is the new brain. It is only available, though, when the "fear"

machine of our old brain is idling. Once your old brain gets revved up, new ideas are hard to come by.

Many leaders today lament the lack of creativity in their organizations. Yet they continue to behave in ways that elicit old brain responses. When people are in the midst of an emotional response to a punitive boss or environment, the probability of creative thinking is pretty low. When you and your team are working with your new brains, you are much more likely to get the best that people have to offer.

As you can see, the behaviors associated with the new brain are the behaviors that we value most in the workplace. If you are looking for clear thinking, solid goal setting and planning, effective communication, creative solutions, and thinking outside the box, it's your new brain you will call upon.

Balance and Adaptation Are Critical

While we are never really totally disengaged from either portion of our brain, the way we balance them is important. The extent to which your old brain is agitated is the extent to which your new brain is constrained.

One might be tempted at this juncture to take a good brain/bad brain stance here. That, of course, would reflect some old brain thinking in itself! The fact is, it is not that the old brain is bad and the new brain is good. We don't get to choose to ignore one in favor of the other and probably would not choose if we could. It may seem counterintuitive, but it is our old brain that ultimately does the choosing. Without the emotional "inclination" provided by our old brain, our analyses would be just that, analytical, not decisive.

Our new brain analyzes.
Our old brain chooses.

Everyone will regularly slip into old brain responding under certain circumstances. Some of us will do it more frequently, others less. The critical challenge is to create effective adaptations that enable us to recover from old brain eruptions that are unhelpful or even disruptive, and forestall them in situations where they will be most destructive. The better we are able to do this, the more we are able to enjoy the value of the old brain as well as the new.

It is helpful to learn techniques that allow you to move back and forth with a modicum of control. Keep in mind, from the discussions above, that the tools we have for tackling our thinking challenges are available through our conscious thought, in our intentions, in our ability to focus consciously and intentionally. These tools don't really apply in an overt or direct way to old brain processes.

When you put all of this together, a couple of critical implications become clear.

* First, *great leadership starts with managing yourself and your own old brain reactions and responses.* In every situation, look first to make sure *you* are bringing your best to the table. Strive to invite and allow your new brain to run the show.

* Second, *the great leader will strive to help those around him/her bring their best to the table.* Do your best to allow and draw out in others their new brain behavior, minimizing obvious old brain interference that is not helpful.

Great leaders first manage themselves, then help others bring their best to the table.

As you already know, this is not easy. Our task going forward is to provide a well informed, scientifically sound picture of the human that shows up for work. This, of course, includes you. So far we have a picture of some of the fundamental drivers of contemporary behavior, with solid roots in our evolutionary past.   The   new brain/old brain   distinction   is one that will serve us well as we continue to fill in this picture.

It will be helpful if we also look at some brain processes in a slightly different way to shed more light on some of the ways our old brain leads into sub-optimal behavior. The next chapter talks about stress and recuperation, and punishment and reward in practical terms.

To accomplish great things, we must not only act, but also dream; not only plan, but also believe.
--Anatole France

3.
The Carrot And The Stick

Over the years, as we have talked to clients in a variety of businesses and at a variety of levels within these businesses, we often ask the question, "How do you know when you are doing a good job?" It will come as no surprise that the most common answer, across many years and many organizations, is, "As long as nobody is complaining, I must be doing okay."

"Have a nice day, Dear."

Many, perhaps most, companies have a culture that is more focused on what is wrong than what is right. There is actually some old brain explanation for this, which we will address in Chapter 4.

This fact of organizational culture, and we believe it to be fact, highlights the importance of two key concepts that come into play in business. The first of these is the experience of stress in the workplace. The second is the use of punishment in our dealings with each other. Let's take a closer look at these two concepts and link them to the old brain.

Business today is nothing if not stressful. Most professionals work more than 50 hours per week, not including what responsibilities we have at home with our families or in our communities. Many of us work far more than this. Stress management is a common topic around both the dinner table and the conference table. Work life balance is on most people's list of things they want to improve in their lives.

"You'll experience a certain amount of stress in your new job, but don't worry. We keep a defibrillator here on my desk."

Our experience shows that the leadership behaviors we present later in this book will help alleviate your stress and help you create an environment that is less stressful for your people. For now, let's understand what is going on a little better.

Ebb and Flow in the Brain

When we are under stress or threat, our bodies, starting with our brains, prepare to respond. As we learned in Chapter 1, most of this preparation is pre-conscious, operating without our awareness. When we examine the evolutionary basis for this we see a sensible process. It looks something like this:

- We sense a threat.
- Our brain sets in motion a series of arousal processes.
- Chemicals in our brain and body shift to facilitate threat responses.
- We respond to the threat by fighting, fleeing, or freezing.
- The threat recedes.
- Our brains and the rest of our body processes the stress chemicals.
- We return to our normal state.

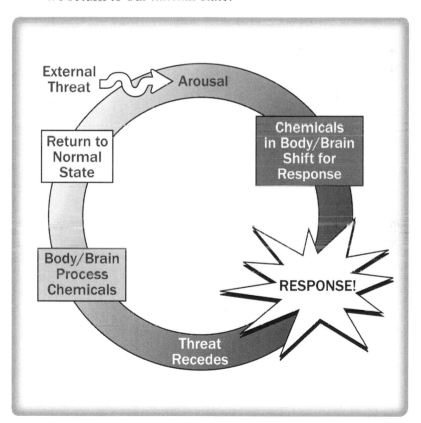

A critical element here is the chemical mix in the brain. Bear with a bit of technical explanation, please!

These chemicals called neurotransmitters are the key to communication among brain cells, called neurons. The space between two connecting neurons is called a synapse. Nerve impulses, which are the communication between brain cells, are dependent on specific chemicals in the small space of the synapse, called the synaptic cleft. The way this works is that one cell, the "sender" cell if you will, releases a small amount of a neurotransmitter into the synaptic cleft by opening small pores on the cell surface in the synapse.

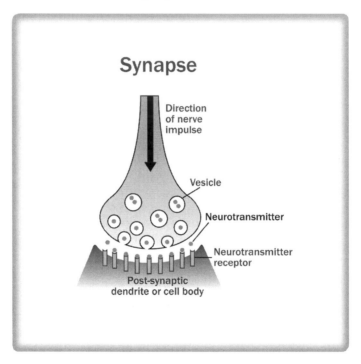

There are a host of different neurotransmitters. You may have heard of epinephrine (adrenaline), dopamine (a "feel good" chemical), serotonin, or norepinephrine. There are many, many chemicals at play within this process. Some of these neurotransmitters serve to excite, others to suppress. Some are associated with feelings of comfort and safety; others are associated with stress and threat.

At any given moment, there is typically only one neurotransmitter operating in a given synapse. As the sender neuron releases a neurotransmitter into the synapse, the molecules migrate across the very small distance to the other neuron. This initiates a chemical reaction in this neuron, or "receptor," cell. At this point the "communication" has happened. One neuron has elicited a response from a neighboring neuron.

The neurotransmitter that was released into the synapse just doesn't stay there. Nor does it just seep into the rest of the brain. The neuron that emitted the neurotransmitter reopens the pores and takes the chemical back in. That is, there is a process called "re-uptake" that clears the synapse and allows it (after a brief recovery period) to transmit again.

As this process happens across thousands and even millions of cells, the particular neurotransmitter in certain parts of the brain is present in quantity in moments of stress or threat. As the threat subsides, then, the re-uptake process removes the influence of these chemicals.

There is a natural ebb and flow of various chemicals in our brain. Some of these make us feel good. Some are associated with more negative experiences, like stress or threat. These chemicals served an adaptive purpose in enabling us to face the threats in our more primitive environment. They still operate in this way today.

Stress and Recovery

As our ancestors faced their primitive environment, threats came and went. That is, Gur and his clan weren't running from lions all day and night. In fact, the threats, though severe, were relatively infrequent. So Gur might walk for hours gathering berries. He might go for days without threat. Suddenly, he sees, or hears, or smells, a predator. He runs as fast as he is able to a safe place. Once there, with the threat removed, he can calm down. That is, his brain can engage in the re-uptake process necessary to restore his brain chemistry to its normal, calm state.

This process takes a little time and is a gradual one. The kind of arousal that led Gur to run can start up quite quickly, but it takes longer to subside. There is a natural ebbing of all the arousing chemicals.

The ebb and flow for Gur, then, was built on a pattern of infrequent, short periods of intense arousal. In between are longer periods of relative calm. This can be depicted with an "arousal curve."

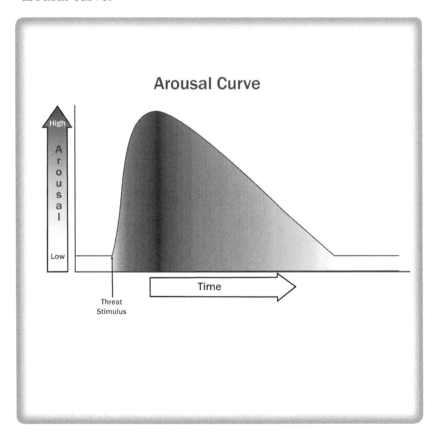

You can think of the height of the curve as a reflection of the extent to which the old brain is driving. The chemicals associated with stress and threat are the chemicals that are involved in the activation of your old brain.

Now, let us compare this pattern to that of a contemporary executive. A typical executive, let's call him Mark, sees danger and mistakes at every turn. Mark feels strongly that his success is dependent upon how he approaches his work. He must wake with the sun and work well into the night to meet his objectives. He must agitate his people to do the same. He must cancel his vacation to attend a critical meeting. He must work during the weekend to insure the survival of his business.

Let's look at Mark's arousal curve.

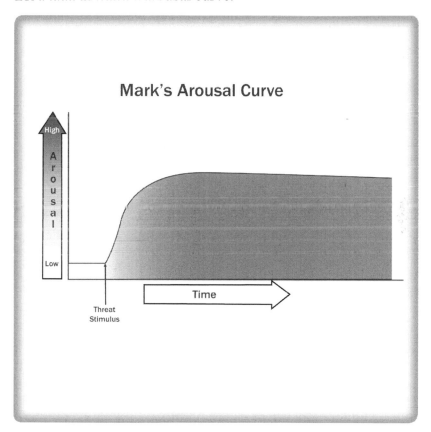

Where is Mark's re-uptake time? His body is wired to experience the chemical mix associated with stress or threat for *short periods of time*. Yet his life is structured to put that mix into play most of the time rather than just occasionally. When this mix is allowed to remain in action for extended periods, unfortunate things begin to happen to Mark's body. He begins to experience "stress" as we know it today. This "stress" is really the accumulated effect of lack of recovery time.

You don't need to be a neurologist to understand that agitation and recovery are a natural cycle. Agitation happens much more quickly than recovery. If you violate this ebb and flow, there is a price to pay. The bigger the violation, the bigger the price. Mark is headed down a road to ulcers, premature aging or even a heart attack.

In later chapters we will talk about actions you can take, such as taking a "time out," that can help you manage this ebb and flow.

Punishment and Reinforcement

There are few areas where leaders show a greater lack of understanding of human behavior as in the application of punishment. We know that the old brain can lead us into sub-optimal behavior. Reliance on punishment as a leadership tool is one example of sub-optimal behavior.

Most of us use punishment and reinforcement as a way to shape the behavior of those around us. We even use reinforcement and punishment to shape our own behavior. If we understand what punishment and reinforcement are, and what consequences follow them, we will be in a position to make better choices as a leader and as a person.

There are two kinds of reinforcement, positive and negative. Both are helpful in changing behavior toward more positive results. You may be surprised by their definitions.

- *Positive reinforcement* is the application of an appetitive stimulus, that is, something that feels good in some sense and therefore something for which we have an appetite. If, immediately after we say or do something, we receive positive reinforcement, we are more likely to say or do that thing  again, we are more likely to do it sooner, or more often, or more easily, or with more intensity. In other words, we pursue those things for which we have an appetite.

- *Negative reinforcement* is the removal of an aversive stimulus, that is something that feels bad or uncomfortable. If, immediately after we say or do something, we do *not* receive something we did *not want* to receive, we are reinforced to say or do it again, sooner, more often, more easily, or with more intensity.

Negative reinforcement is NOT punishment!!

For example, you decide to tell your boss some really bad news, even though you anticipate that he will yell at you when he hears it. You enter his office and blurt out the bad news. Your boss is quiet for a moment, then says "Sit down, please, and give me a moment to think about this. And thank you for bringing it to my attention so quickly." You have just received *negative reinforcement* to speak more openly to your boss.

As you can see, both positive and negative reinforcement work in essentially the same way. Whatever is occurring *immediately before* the application of the appetitive stimulus, or the removal or prevention of the aversive stimulus, is reinforced.

Applying an appetitive stimulus - for example, saying to someone, "Nice job you did there" - reinforces that nice job. Removing an aversive stimulus - as in moving someone out of a dirty, noisy work environment immediately after they have made a reasonable business case for this move - works in the same way, reinforcing the making of reasonable businesses cases. In doing these reinforcing things, we are encouraging, at the neurological level, some particular behaviors. This works whether we are doing so intentionally or not.

Punishment is different. It is the application of an aversive stimulus. That is, we apply some stimulus that hurts or is uncomfortable, or doesn't feel good in some way. Whatever is happening immediately before the application of the aversive stimulus will be less likely to occur, will occur less frequently, or will occur with less intensity. Here, we have discouraged, at the neurological level, a broad range of behaviors. If Little Billy gets smacked at the dinner table for swinging his foot into the table leg, in one instant he may build an aversion to the table, the chair, the room, the food in front of him, the smells around him, the music playing in the background, the day of the week, and the person who smacked him. The chemical reaction to punishment is not specific, as in the case of reinforcement, but wide reaching and non-specific.

We typically do not get to see much new brain behavior from a person who has been punished.

It would be easy to assume at this point that punishment is the opposite of reinforcement. This is not the case. There are critical differences in these ways of shaping behavior.

There are some similarities. How are punishment and rein-forcement the same? They will both shape the behavior of an organism, any organism. Our interest here is people, more specifically people at work. But this shaping applies to all animals. It is possible to use reinforcement and punishment to shape the behavior of even single celled organisms.

So, if your goal is *simply and exclusively to shape behavior*, with no concern for other consequences, there is no difference between reinforcement and punishment to speak of. However, the long-term consequences of using punishment are serious and, frankly, potentially debilitating to business.

A major difference between reinforcement and punishment is the extent to which they activate old brain responses. Punishment is much more likely than reinforcement to elicit the kinds of behaviors we will investigate further in a later chapter: fight, flight, or freeze. We typically don't see a lot of new brain behavior when people are being punished.

In addition, because of the power of the old brain to activate immediate behavior, punishment works very quickly. When you apply an aversive stimulus, people stop doing what they were doing, right away

Here's what's unfortunate. This immediate modification of behavior after the application of punishment is *reinforcing to the punisher.* Immediately after the punisher jumps on someone, the person being punished responds in a way that means "Never again!" This is what the punisher wanted, so punishing behavior is reinforced. It may be clear now why punishment has become a way of life to many.

A second major difference between reinforcement and punishment is specificity. Reinforcement is very focused and specific. Smiling at someone when they come to your office door will have the effect of bringing people to your open door more readily, nothing more.

> Punishing behavior is reinforcing to the
> punisher. While the punished individual is
> quickly responding in ways to stop
> the aversive stimulus, the punisher is
> experiencing reinforcement to do it again.

Punishment is broader and more generalized. A simple example, unfortunately familiar to most of us, is a dog that has been abused by its owner. We usually recognize the behavior and label it quickly. What is it that we see that leads us to the conclusion of abuse? The dog's head will drop down with no eye contact. The tail will be drawn between the dog's legs. The dog will hunch over and skulk around. He will not approach you directly. Rather, he will circle, keeping furniture between you and him.

Why would the dog do this when you have never done anything to harm the animal? Simply put, the effects of punishment received from someone else generalize quickly and easily, in ways we often do not anticipate. The effects generalize not only to other people. They also generalize to similar situations, places, time of day, and so forth.

In business, when someone is punished, he will not only stop doing what he is doing, he will likely develop negative feelings about his boss, about his company, and just about anything else even remotely associated with the situation. The negativity generated by this punishment pervades a workplace, to no good end. We sometimes refer to this as bad morale.

On the other hand, we see very specific positive responses to reinforcement.   If our goal is to do our best, and be our best, and to help others around us do the same, it seems a clear choice.

Reinforcement is far superior as a leadership tool.

There is an exception to the "never punish" rule. If you have absolutely unacceptable behavior that *cannot* be tolerated under any circumstances because of its very nature, and you want it to stop right away, punishment will give you what you want. Some examples in the workplace include bringing a loaded weapon to work, use or distribution of illegal drugs in the workplace, dangerous work behavior such as inappropriate use of a blowtorch, and assaulting a coworker. Fortunately, these are rare occurrences.

Punishment is guaranteed to get you an old brain response.

This cannot be reinforced strongly enough! *Punishment is a tool of last resort.* In practically every situation, reinforcement will get you more of what you want, from yourself and from others.

Let's say it again: Reinforcement is the preferred tool. Using punishment almost always means that you have given up and given in to your old brain. You will be rewarded if you exhaust your reinforcement options before you resort to your last alternative of punishment.

Punishment is a tool of last resort. Exhaust your reinforcement options before you even consider it.

4.
The Persistent Pursuit of Problems

As mentioned previously, when we ask business people, "How do you know when you are doing a good job?" the most common response is, "I know I'm doing a good job when no one is chewing me out." It is indeed a serious testament to the power of our old brain that success is so often defined simply as the absence of failure.

As we have already seen, our old brain is exquisitely tuned to attend and respond to threat. In the contemporary world, threats are no longer rustles in the bushes. Rather, they look like problems at work, mistakes by subordinates, and our own individual shortfalls. And, admit it, we especially relish the mistakes of others.

Before we can avoid the errors of business (mistakes, bad judgment, failure of execution, poor planning), we can best be served by understanding how we are drawn so relentlessly to problems and threats around us, and the shortcomings of others.

When your New Brain for Business is in charge, attention is on success rather than failure. The tenor is positive rather than negative. A primary leadership challenge is to see through the negative noise and seize the successes that surround us most of the time. How do we exert leverage over our old brain to make this shift? Let's look at a couple of real life examples.

Treasure Your Problems?

Consider Walt, the head of a refinery operations facility responsible for billions of dollars in operating revenue. Every Monday morning, Walt conducts a staff meeting, where he reviews 52 pages of facility metrics with his direct reports.

Not everything that counts can be counted, and not everything that can be counted counts.
--Albert Einstein

Walt's typical approach to this data sounds like this: "I see catalyst utilization is 2% over plan this week. What's going on there?" Or, "I thought we had contractor head count below 80!" Walt delivers these comments and questions in a calm, friendly manner. When questioned about what he hopes to accomplish by focusing only on the negatives, he responds with bromides like, "You treasure what you measure." And, indeed, Walt treasures his problems.

But wait! We do have to hit certain metrics to know we are running our business successfully, right? Of course we do! But there are literally thousands of data points in Walt's 52 pages of metrics, and the only ones he focuses on are the ones that are *off spec*. What about all the metrics that say this business is being run well? What are the true implications of those that are "off spec?" How is the business running, truly?

Walt has been drawn in by the siren song of problems. His old brain is running the show.

A good decision is based on knowledge and not on numbers.
--Plato

What is the impact of this approach on his team? Can we make a connection between this negative, problem focused leadership and the operating challenges that Walt is facing in his plant?

Imagine you are one of Walt's direct reports. How do you approach the Monday morning meeting? Walt's people keep their heads down and hope Walt badgers someone else. If they do end up tied to the whipping post, they often have a well rehearsed story about how it was someone else's fault, or how things are going to be better in the future, even if their story distorts reality. When working with a boss like Walt, people typically want to make sure that any problems showing up in their area are *someone else's fault* wherever possible.

These are the responses we should expect. When Walt lets his old brain do the driving, he is going to get old brain behavior from his team. We are not surprised when we learn that Walt is struggling to keep his plant fully operational, because nobody is looking forward. They are all trying to manage Walt's attention on their own areas by chasing mistakes. There is plenty of "silo"

behavior as every-
one tries to stay out
of Walt's crosshairs
by shifting respon-
sibility onto others.

Here is what Walt
says:"These metrics
are absolutely criti-
cal for driving the
performance of the
plant.   We know
that when we pay
attention to these
metrics, the plant
runs better.   The
biggest problem I have to deal with is that people aren't chasing
the metrics hard enough."

Walt is convinced of the rightness of focusing on mistakes and
problems. This feeling of rightness about his negative approach
is the manifestation of his old brain exerting influence. It feels
natural and correct for Walt to blame his team for problems. So,
the breakdowns, turf wars, and blame games are problems that
reside, from the perspective of Walt's old brain, with his plant
directors. For now, we need only keep in mind that this is just
the natural result of Walt's over-playing his old brain
adaptations.

Lest Walt starts feeling too special, let's remember that he is
certainly not the only leader to fall victim to this siren song.
Here is another real life example.

Fighter Jet Leadership

Doug is the CEO and president of a vertically integrated food
products company. With production, distribution, and retail
sales under one company, there are plenty of opportunities for

problems with product quality, cost control, and customer satisfaction. Doug's main complaint is that no one seems willing to take ownership of things outside their own area.

Doug's leadership style could best be described as "the fighter jet." No one sees him until he dives in from behind a cloud with a roar, strafes the troops, and zooms off back into the clouds, leaving the dazed and wounded to recover on their own. With his old brain firmly seated in the cockpit, Doug takes aim at every mistake made anywhere on the value chain. When he takes aim, he fires freely. He is famous throughout the company for his profanity-laced tirades that question the motives, abilities, and character of members of his team.

Doug is a very confusing boss for his team. When he is engaged personally with others, he is funny, friendly, and compassionate. He seems to know everyone, their spouses and children. He is known for going out of his way to help when employees are struggling (providing a vehicle to drive after a car accident, sending people home when a child is sick, visiting an employee's mother in the hospital). When he talks about his passion for the company, people feel inspired. And he pays a fair wage.

Typically, however, Doug is absent from day-to-day operations, so people see more of his fighter jet approach, and no one wants to be raked with his gunfire.

People dread meetings with Doug. Instead of agendas, the meetings are driven by Doug's current peeves. He pounces from problem to problem, taking aim, blasting away, then moving on. His team struggles to predict where he will attack next.

People live in fear of being in Doug's sights. Demonstrating a willingness to take ownership of anything, they will tell you, simply increases the number of targets on your back for Doug to shoot at! The team lives in a state of constantly elevated anxiety: their old brains are more active than is helpful, both when Doug is around and when he is not. Let's face it, this is just not much fun.

The story crafted at the behest of Doug's old brain is different from Walt's, but just as powerful. "I am passionate about the pursuit of excellence! Nothing serves our clients better than this, and it is the only way I can see to ensure the long term success of the company! Unfortunately, others lack my passion and focus, so I have to stay on them about it."

"I am passionate in the pursuit of excellence!"

He views his tirades as the best way to energize and focus people on the critical issues of the moment. He feels fully justified in his actions because they match his story, which makes sense to him. It feels comfortable and right. The problems reside with others. He is doing the right things, with a lot of intensity provided by his old brain.

Sing That Siren's Song

What is really going on with these two leaders? Both Walt and Doug want great business results. Both of them really care about what they do. Both believe they are doing what they can to increase success.

A boss creates fear, a leader confidence.
--Russell H. Ewing

The short answer is that they have gotten lost in their own old brain behavior. A longer answer is that they are pulled by their old brain's primal focus on danger, to which they react. When something doesn't look or feel right to them, they immediately react to the danger of failure in the business at a very fundamental, unconscious level. What was once truly adaptive, helpful behavior now creates a blanket of negativity that keeps these leaders and their people from doing their best work.

Walt and Doug aren't stupid. They are intelligent, accomplished, successful business leaders. How is it that they can't see what is happening here? Each has his own story about why he feels he is doing what is necessary and right. Neither of them is intentionally choosing to create a negative, mistake focused environment. They aren't intentionally choosing to create fear, avoidance, blaming, or silo-building behavior in their teams. Yet, it is their behavior that is the driver for these reactions and results, every day.

Our old brain quickly draws our attention to threat, danger and failure.

The single most valuable contribution of the old brain in helping us survive is its ability to rapidly orient us to risk and danger in the environment around us.

This is the reason that bad news sells newspapers – our attention is drawn to the threatening headline. This is the reason we slow down in traffic, even if the wreck is on the other side of the freeway. We are unable *not* to look. How can you ignore the blurb on the TV, "Toxic gas leak! Tune in at 11 and see if you are going to die!"

In our evolutionary past, there was huge value to our ability as individuals to spot these situations and make an adjustment in our behavior to increase our survivability, and to do so very quickly. So, we have a very, very, *very* strong bias to focus on what is *wrong*. Paying attention to what is going right gets moved further down the agenda. Often it doesn't make the agenda at all.

In contemporary business, this takes the form of identifying mistakes in the space around us. Leaders regularly focus on what is *not* working. Actually, so does everyone else! We have strong reactions and put our complete focus on fixing specific mistakes. Even though we tell ourselves to dish out the "atta-boys" and pats on the back, and we can talk about the value of celebrating our successes, we are driven to focus on the negative. Many of us have to set up reminders to do the positive reinforcement that plays such a critical role in helping others be and do their best.

Check your own calendar for the last week or two and see how you have spent your time. How much is problem focused? Review your most recent meeting agenda. What are the top two or three items? There is no need to feel guilty about this - it is what we are wired to do. We are fulfilling the destinies that are genetically

Agenda
1. Plant Explosion
2. SEC Investigation
3. Stockholder Revolt
4. Product Tampering
5. Disgruntled Employees

mapped into our brain. Shifting this balance between a negative versus positive focus is really swimming upstream against our evolutionary imperatives.

When our old brains are charged up, we are often among the last to notice. Others may see our agitation before we see it ourselves. Surely you have watched someone "lose their cool" and wondered how they can't see it for themselves? Here's how: what they are doing *feels right, normal, and natural to them.*

The old brain is very good at helping us feel "normal" even when we are riled up. If we didn't have this strong feeling of being right, we would find it much easier to let go, move on, or get over it. The *feeling of rightness* is a fundamental and powerful phenomenon within our brain functioning that often prevents us from being our best.

It is critical to keep in mind this notion of feeling fully justified. None of us feels or believes that we engage in random or evil behavior. We grant ourselves the best of intentions. We need only keep in mind that Walt and Doug will not be easily diverted from their problem focus because that focus feels right and safe for them.

Everyone feels fully justified!

Yet, it is clear that each of these leaders is sowing the seeds of his own suboptimal business performance. In fact, our ability to use our new brain as we look at these two leaders allows us to see what they cannot. We are not, in viewing their behavior, constrained by our old brains. Our success is not threatened by their behavior. Our sense of self-esteem is not at risk.

In our own businesses, the challenge of resisting this siren song is just as daunting as in it for Walt and Doug.

What Can You Do?

You may ask, why is this only the job of the leader? Why can't Walt's people pay more attention to the metrics?   Why can't Doug's people take more ownership of the company's success?

We all have an old brain that keeps us attending to problems and threats. It keeps us safe and continues to help us survive. In our daily lives, however, we repeatedly fall prey to its siren song, luring us to focus on what's wrong, in ways that play out poorly for us. As a leader, your behavior has a big impact on how well others are able to overcome their old brain drivers.

Here are some actions you can take to overcome your strong and natural tendency to look primarily for failure. You can start right now to balance this strong drive and increase your positive impact as a leader.

• **Tell People What You Want, Not What You Don't Like**

   Most of the time, spending energy thinking and talking about what we do not like is not helpful, and in fact tends to take us into serious old brain territory. In order to have a positive impact on the running of your business, spend more time clarifying what you truly want, and communicate it to others. Sometimes, the best thing to do with what you do not like is to ignore it.

   When a problem arises and immediately gets our attention, pointing out what is wrong is an easy trap in which to fall. Take a moment to think about what you would have liked to have seen, had all gone well. Once you have a clear picture of that in your mind, share it. Describe this picture of what it might have looked like to those who will be involved, so they are clear about your expectations. Leave it to them, unless you have a very good reason not to, to determine the difference between this description and what actually happened. It allows the individual to see a picture of their successful self, even after a potential failure.

A very good reason not to do this is if there is physical danger in the problem being repeated. Very few other reasons to dwell in the past are good reasons.

• Focus on What Is Going Well

Every day, find at least one person who is behaving in a way that you believe supports the success of the business and tell them about it.

Here is an example. One day, Robert was in his office when he heard Evelyn, an administrative employee, on the telephone. She was clearly dealing with an unhappy customer, and yet her voice was calm. There were long periods of silence while she apparently listened closely, and she asked clarifying questions. At the end of the call, she outlined very specifically the step-by-step actions she would take to resolve the customer's issue, including timelines.

Robert was pleased to have heard her in action, and he went to her cubicle at once. He asked her to tell him about the call. She confirmed that the customer had been upset, but that she felt he had calmed down by the end of the call. Robert pointed out what he had noticed, then smiled. "We have made a promise to our customers that we will do what we say we will do, and sometimes we slip. You assured this customer that he will get what he expected from us, and that is all we can do when things don't go as we planned. Thank you for keeping our promise."

Obviously, Robert would have preferred that everything had been perfect and the customer was not upset. But realistically, neither business nor life works that way. In this case, Robert reinforced to himself as well as to Evelyn that the way they handled problems was as critical as the way they handled success.

- ## Follow the 10:1 Rule

  Because the electronic pathways between our emotional brain and our intentional brain are weighted so heavily toward emotion, offsetting the impact is critical. If you are not already doing this, begin now!   For each person with whom you want a better relationship and from whom you would like better results, have *ten* "positive" interactions for every *one* "negative" one.

  Positive interactions include behaviors that are simple (saying hello in the morning), regular (asking how things are going), easy (listening effectively), and consistent (recognizing positive performance). Negative interactions include ignoring the other person, focusing on problems, criticizing performance, and making wisecracks at the person's expense, to name a few.

  Stephen Covey, in his book *The 7 Habits of Highly Effective People,* captured this well in recommending the Emotional Bank Account.   If you have enough positive "savings," people will allow some withdrawals and see them as evidence that you are human.   If the account balance goes negative, they are more likely to confuse your behavior with your intentions and begin to respond to you with a lot of old brain energy.

- ## Separate Business from Personal

  The old brain will be less problem focused when you separate an analysis of the business from any review of performance.   Both Doug and Walt fell into the trap of making business results into something personal.   In their own ways, each saw their employees as failures - not enough passion, not enough attention to the right things. If you are viewing "people" in a certain negative way, you have likely found a story that supports your old brain's attention to problems.

Business is business. Metrics provide us with a picture of the business that can stimulate sound, solid, analytical thinking. Look over the metrics and reach your own conclusions or clarify your own confusions. Avoid asking "why" ("Why is contractor head count over 80?") and ask people to do good thinking. "What will it take to get contractor head count below 80, and what are the implications of doing that?"

• Conduct an Intentional Leadership Conversation

If you find you are dealing with an issue specifically associated with one person, turn the conversation into one where the two of you are investigating how each of you can be your best. An intentional leadership conversation is one where you are taking great care to think through what is really happening in the conversation, to reach positive ends.

Here is a "mental model" you can use to be more intentional in your conversations. A mental model or "thinking model," is intended to help you prepare for something, in this case a meaningful conversation with someone.

This model can be used simply for delivery of a message, although with potentially less desirable results. Because of the difficulty of demonstrating the model any other way, however, here is an example of how it can be used for delivering a message to an employee, Chuck, who consistently arrives late to work. On the left is a description of the discussion - elements of the intentional leadership conversation - that can take place to focus on improving performance without dipping into old brain territory. On the right is an example of "delivery," although a full interactive discussion will of course work much better.

Mental Model: *What is our goal?*
Share your thinking about the business purpose for the action or behavior. Investigate why what this person is doing really matters. Make the connection to the larger vision. This helps people understand how their behavior fits into a larger picture of success. It also draws their attention to the future, which reduces old brain activity.

> **Example "Delivery":**
> "Chuck, our promise to our clients is that we are available to them at certain times of the day. Our promise to each other is that we have each others' backs when we get overloaded. When we keep these promises, we tend to have fun and do great work."

Mental Model: *What behavior will work better?*
Discuss and reach agreement on the specific behavior desired. Assume that they will figure out on their own what you want them to do. Do not spend much time talking about the behavior you are getting now that you do not like, unless it is the only way the other person can understand the contrast of current vs. desired behavior.

> **Example "Delivery":**
> "Because you are in charge of the office, your being here on time is sometimes the only way we can ensure that we are keeping these promises. As you know, the phone is often ringing first thing in the morning. Many of us are out with clients on a regular basis. So we are all - clients and team members - counting on you to be here to respond to these needs immediately and to keep us all on track."

Mental Model: *What good will happen if the new behavior works as expected?*

Investigate the positive consequences that are expected to follow when the behavior is demonstrated. This allows the other person to understand that he or she has "success" under his or her control. Remembering how reinforcement works, positive consequences define successful behavior.

> **Example "Delivery":**
> "If you are here, ready to work, at 8:00 every morning, those who are out with clients will know they can count on you for help. They will be better able to do their work. Clients will call and reach someone, and feel we are there to serve them, and will feel better about working with us. All of us will better appreciate how critical you are to the team."

Mental Model: *Ask for commitment.*
Ask for (and make) a public commitment to engage in the specific behavior desired.

> **Example "Delivery":**
> "Can I get your commitment that you will be in the office, ready to answer the phone and respond to requests for help at 8:00 every morning?"

Let us assume that Chuck agreed to be at work on time, and began to demonstrate his commitment immediately. You can now use this as an opportunity to build up your emotional bank account with him. It does require paying attention to Chuck's changing behavior, which is the only way you can reinforce it.

When you see Chuck showing up on time or even early, you can thank him for being there and reinforce to him how this clearly sends a message of teamwork and client commitment. You can ask him about calls he has received and how he had responded to them, pointing out how he was a critical member of the team in handling these calls. Finally, you can ask how he is doing. The combination of his new behavior and your attention in positively reinforcing it can lead to immediate results that can be sustained over time.

• Clarify What's Important

Deciding what is really important is a key responsibility of a leader. There are always many, many distractions to successfully running your business. It is easier to be distracted by them if you have not thought through what you want to accomplish, decided what it will take to accomplish it, and then paid close attention to what is happening. The first step - thinking through what you want to accomplish - is often the easiest!

Where possible, invite others to think about what key benchmarks are worth paying attention to. Facilitate one or more meaningful discussions about this and reach agreement on those key benchmarks.

Now you can pay attention to them yourself, just as others are paying attention. The "treasure what you measure" concept was never intended as a metrics club but rather a reminder of natural human behavior. Choose the few things that you can and will attend to. Pursue them until you achieve what you want or until there is a really good reason to stop pursuing them. This leads to better and faster results.

• Monitor Your Own Old Brain Behavior

Identify the cues that indicate you have been seduced by the persistent pursuit of problems. Often, the cue will be someone else's pointing to something as a failure. It is also common that we get stuck attending to a problem that really isn't important anymore, although it used to be. Use these cues as triggers to help yourself get to an alternate approach.

Take feedback seriously, even if you do not understand it. People won't always tell you what you want to hear, but they will often tell you what you need to know.

Ask for cue or trigger information ("I do tend to react when I am interrupted too much. Do you see me reacting like this at other times?"). Ask people what they want to have happen instead ("What can I do to feel confident that this work will be done?").

Pay attention to what you say and do. Even if you don't catch yourself until too late, use it to reinforce to yourself when you can do something differently.

If you expect this to be easy, you will be disappointed! Give yourself a break - but practice, practice, practice.

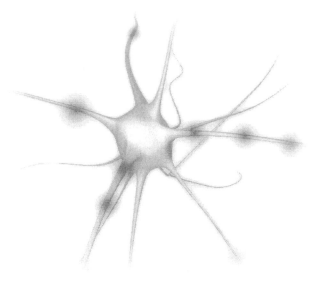

5.
The Tiny Tool Chest

When we take on a tough business challenge, it is important that we "bring our A Game." By this we mean our most critical thinking, our best analysis, our clearest communication. Unfortunately, when the challenge evokes an emotional response from us (and what real business challenge doesn't?), our A Game is usually not available to us. When we get emotionally agitated and our old brain starts doing more of the driving, we are left with just a few simple responses. You could call this the Tiny Tool Chest.

There have already been many references to Gur and his clan members taking certain action in specific situations -- running at the prospect of a predator in the bushes, for example.   The fact is that we truly only have three response choices when our old brain takes complete charge. If we become so fearful or angry that we are completely on auto-pilot, we will either freeze, flee or fight.

This is an extremely limited tool chest and yet it served us well in a primitive environment. It continues to serve us well even now, if we are suddenly physically threatened. The environments we live in now are not primitive, however, and they are quite sophisticated and complex. They require commensurate complexity and sophistication in our responses, responses for which our old brain is much less well adapted.

The good news is that most of the time we find ourselves in situations where our old brains do not take complete control. Our new brains are usually involved to some extent. But, there are still too many situations where leaders settle for fight, flight, or freeze in themselves, and in those around them. Examining how these three basic response models operate in the contemporary world of work can help us all become better leaders.

Don't Move!

Probably the most common of our tools is freezing. Stan, a manufacturing manager at a large manufacturing plant, was known for his foul language and aggressive style. He felt people needed to "step up and take what I dish out" because "how else will we hit our production goals?"

Each week, Stan had a meeting of his direct reports to talk about what had happened the week before and what would happen in the upcoming week. He had a keen mind and he could calculate complicated relationships in his head quickly, so it was not unusual for him to show up with a stack of reports and flip through them, shooting questions at his people like a pellet gun.

Over time, people became accustomed to the process, and as long as they were prepared, they responded to Stan's questions and the discussion moved on. People were always on guard, however, for Stan to ask a question to which they had no answer. When this happened, Stan was ruthless in his attacks on the leader who did not come prepared.

As soon as Stan's vilification began, everyone else in the room had a common reaction - they froze. No more sidebar conversations, no "chipmunking" on their smart phone. Eyes down, people just sat very still with the hope they would not get noticed.

If Stan asked another question of another leader, he typically got monosyllabic answers from people, sending the message "not me, not me!" Stan's behavior resulted in others shutting down, and his frustration peaked because he didn't understand why people were not engaging with him!

It is important to understand that Stan's conduct permeated beyond the borders of the meeting room. The impact was very detrimental to this plant. People began to avoid each other and Stan, stopped talking to each other about critical events, and looked for ways to stay out of the limelight. Stan found himself regularly surprised by bad news, because people tried to hide and fix issues without his knowing and reacting.

The team also missed the opportunity to increase their capability by helping each other solve problems more effectively. Because of the danger posed by Stan's approach, people kept their heads down when good analytical conversation would have served everyone better. Even when people tried to overcome their tendency to avoid interaction, they limited information and colluded on the quick solution to avoid the surfacing of a problem. Overall, the plant ran suboptimally under Stan's leadership.   Stan's attacks were so frightening to people that he triggered a powerful response from the old brain's tiny tool chest.

Flee the Scene

A second but equally powerful tool in our tool chest is flight. When we are frightened, a proven method of survival is to run away.   Typically in today's workforce situations, running away is not commonly required because the challenge is not physically threatening.   This does not mean, however, that we do not flee the scene in other ways.

Ted is the regional executive of a large financial services firm. He is responsible for half of the company's business. He is very

talented in his chosen field, and he builds strong, lasting relationships with his clients. He is also seen as a valued leader by his direct reports, who find his counsel regularly directed at their success.   Ted's downfall is his overuse of his one tool, flight. When it appears that someone is unhappy with him, his work or his people, Ted disappears until the cloud has passed over, leaving others to fill in the gap for him.

Examples of this behavior are abundant. Ted frequently excuses himself from meetings when the subject has moved to an arena in which he has been expected to accomplish something but it is not complete. Even if he is not a "failure" but simply does not have good news to report, Ted chooses to plead "call from a client" to remove himself from the conversation.

Ted is also adept at changing the subject, if physically leaving is not possible without giving his strategy of flight away.   He knows the key issues of running the business and can raise critical, helpful questions to move the conversation off of him and onto something less threatening.   Others see his critical questioning as an important contribution, and in fact it is, at least in some situations.   His motivation, though, is really not so beneficial.

The biggest impact of Ted's flight behavior is that difficult and uncomfortable issues do not get resolved.   Ted's people end up feeling frustrated that no matter what Ted tells them he will do, nothing seems to change.   Although he is good at camouflaging his lack of assertively addressing critical issues, over time Ted's staff and peers began to lose faith in his ability to lead.

Make no mistake, there are times when removing oneself from a difficult situation is an appropriate and effective response. When the old brain is driving, though, this is usually a suboptimal solution.

When the withdrawal serves only our own sense of safety rather than the benefit of the business, we are surrendering our powerful new brain thinking to a baser motive. Ted is destined to miss opportunities for growth and success - his, his people's and the firm's - because of his tendency to give in to this baser motive and flee.

Scary Moments

Real fights aren't part of the normal leadership toolkit. If you find yourself in an actual "fight" situation - meaning physical altercation - remove yourself from it as quickly as you can. This is an opportunity for people with special training. Law enforcement and clinical/counseling professionals are the people to look to here.

Let's look at an example.

Sherry, a professional level employee, got agitated one day and began yelling at an administrative colleague and throwing things, including a desk phone and stapler, both heavy objects. The rest of the administrative staff were cowering under their desks when Joan, the office manager, joined the fray. There was little Joan could do to positively influence the situation, although her presence did have a calming effect. She remained calm, and immediately called for security personnel to help her deal with any further "fight" behavior.

The best response to old brain "fight" is avoidance.

In such a situation, at least one old brain was running rampant. Joan did not let her old brain take over. Of course she was agitated, and you would be too. Your old brain will resonate with the threat in the air. The best leadership behavior in this case is to get help. You and your team will be best served if you resist letting a bad situation become a tragic one.

Do not allow a bad situation to become a tragic one.

Limited Response Repertoire

So now we are clear that the old brain has a response repertoire that is extremely limited: fight, flight, or freeze. We have all felt and seen these in action. This continues to be a pretty effective tool kit where the situation demands it. The reality is, though, that situations that demand these types of responses are quite rare in our contemporary lives.

Our biology lags behind our physical and social environment. Some organizations have a high tolerance for "fighting." People yell at each other, use vulgar language, call each other names, pound their fists, perhaps even stomp out of the room and slam the door. Plenty of "fight" here, with this last action as an example of "flight" as well.

Organizations that tolerate this type of behavior tend to end up with cultures that are highly internally competitive. "Winning" against each other becomes acceptable and encouraged. The customer, the employees and the shareholder often get lost in the skirmish.

Internal competition does not serve the customer or the business in the long run.

You may even have found yourself "speechless" or "at a loss for words" at times when the situation triggers some old brain activity. As in Stan's case, organizations that do not attend to

these reactions tend to have suboptimal business results because people are focused on safety, not good business.

In each case, fighting, fleeing or freezing, our responses are *simple*. We are not doing any analytical thinking. We are not being creative, nor are we reaching effective resolution to any problem. We are simply satisfying our old brain's need for taking immediate action in a situation where a threat has been perceived. "If I can

just get high enough up this tree, the predators won't get me."
This is self-preservation, plain and simple.

What Can You Do?

- ### Take a Time Out

  When our old brains are howling, having some time to
  allow ourselves to calm down (to allow time for
  neurotransmitter re-uptake) can make a world of difference.
  Whether it is your own fear response that you catch, or
  someone else's, taking a standing eight count will benefit
  everyone involved.

  "I feel a bad attitude
  coming on. May I take the
  rest of the day off?"

- ### Use the 10:1 Rule

  In Stan's case, he took so little action to make people feel
  safe and appreciated that his attacks were overwhelming.
  Over time, he began to recognize people's efforts and talk to
  them about how well they were doing.

  One of his direct reports likes to tell a story about how, at
  the beginning of his application of the 10:1 Rule, Stan had
  just let loose on one of his people in the weekly meeting

when he suddenly stopped himself. He "fumed" for a few minutes, then seemed to get himself under control. To everyone's surprise, he said "George, I want you to know I think you are doing a good job." Then he continued with the questioning.

Later, several people in the meeting got together and talked about Stan's unusual behavior. They decided to give Stan the benefit of the doubt, thinking that perhaps he meant well even when he didn't behave well. Stan noticed a difference after that, which reinforced his using the 10:1 Rule! The change had begun!

- ## Use Tentative Language

We are in the habit of using "imperative" language regularly. Imperative language, regardless of how casually it is used, has an urgency and criticality to it that reduces our choices. "I need to get this done." "I should pay more attention." "You have to take care of this now." All alternatives have been slammed behind the door of imperatives, so that we feel we have no choice. When we feel we have no choice, our old brain stirs, because having only one choice does not seem safe.

Imperative language can corner people into a fear response. Telling people what they *have* to do or what they *should* do or what they *need* to do is rarely helpful. Allowing people to make their own choices and live with the consequences of them can reduce fear responses and allow for more creative, thoughtful and helpful thinking. Isn't this what we are usually striving for?

Here are some examples of how to turn imperative language into tentative language without giving up important business results:

Imperative	Tentative
I need to get this done.	I want to get this done, because I believe it will lead to good customer service. I think it is important enough that I choose to do it instead of something else.
I should pay more attention to others when they are talking to me.	When I pay more attention to others, I learn more from them and I am able to be more helpful. It probably keeps me from missing important information. When others are talking to me, I will begin to pay more attention.
You have to take care of this now.	If you can take care of this now, this customer will see that we keep our promises.

- ## Use Empathic Responses

  If you see evidence of any of the tools from the tiny tool chest in use, remember that a keen fear is the key trigger. Although you do not have to tolerate inappropriate behavior, responding similarly to others will not be helpful. You can be forceful in bringing a difficult situation to a close and still be kind. One of the most palpable ways you can do this is with empathy.

  Empathy can show up in many ways. At its core is an understanding that people are not at their best every moment, including ourselves, and yet we want to be and even strive to be. When two people enter a situation together, it just might get messy. Keeping yourself above the fray and helping others cope pays off in myriad ways.

  Recognizing and allowing people to have their authentic emotional reactions gives them permission to be human.

Setting the boundaries for any behavior that accompanies those emotions is reasonable and kind.

Be kind, for everyone you meet is fighting a hard battle.
--Plato

Let's imagine that you are dealing with someone who has reached a frustration level that is beginning to show to others. There are a number of ways you can respond with empathy and effectiveness. Here are some examples.

- You might go to him and say, "It is obvious that you are upset and that this is difficult for you. Let's step into my office and see if we can improve the situation." This demonstrates that you care and that you intend to be helpful. It also sets a boundary of where the best place to deal with the situation might be.

- You might go to him and say, "Take a break, Joe. We'll take care of this." This sets a boundary and gives him a chance to calm down. You can also suggest that everyone take a break, if there is a meeting taking place. This allows everyone to relax for a few minutes.

Empathy demonstrates that you understand and care, so this can also work as an added deposit into your Emotional Bank Account with this individual.

Dealing with the Tiny Tool Chest can be very frightening or barely noticeable. People behave in varying ways, some of which show up in the following chapters.

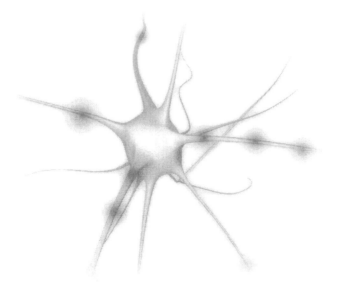

6.
The Game of Blame and Shame

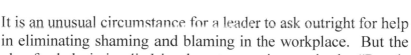

It is an unusual circumstance for a leader to ask outright for help in eliminating shaming and blaming in the workplace. But the plea for help is implied in almost every issue raised. "People won't tell me what I need to know!" "The infighting here has gotten really ugly!" "We would get more done if people would just mind their own business."

None of us likes to be blamed by others, even for mistakes and problems for which we are responsible. The feeling of shame associated with being blamed feels really, really bad. So we avoid it. We put a lot of time and effort into avoiding the shame and blame that surrounds us when something goes wrong. As we look more closely at the shaming and blaming process, we will see what an incredible obstacle to progress it represents.

As leaders, we are at our best when we keep everyone's attention on improvement and success. If we lead in ways that avoid blaming and shaming, we get more openness to learning from mistakes in the future. But we have already pointed out how our natural tendency is to zero in on the mistake or problem.

If the culture of an organization allows and even nurtures blaming and shaming, that company will experience lots of miscommunication, pointing out the errors of others, assigning blame, feeling ashamed, and failing to get work done!

Shame as Motivator

John's story is similar to many, many leaders. He is the CEO of large organization that has had considerable success in the past. However, it is in a difficult line of business and times are hard. So John has instituted a way to keep information in front of his leaders about how they are doing.

John has purchased expensive, extensive, and sophisticated industry standard benchmarks of performance and set the expectation that his company will regularly fall in the top one or two quartiles of these benchmarks. He has regular data provided to his managers about how they are doing and how others in the organization are doing. Any leader in the organization can review the data monthly and see where their results fall, relative to internal peers and relative to other companies. In addition, John has a monthly meeting of his top executives to discuss and better understand the data, as well as to reinforce expectations of results.

© 2008 Ted Goff

"We're looking for someone for the fast-paced and exciting job of blamee."

John has set up the perfect storm for shaming his leaders. When asked, he will explain that his intention is to provide information to his leaders, which allows the organization to analyze business results and make sound decisions. He will also say he expects each function to set their own priorities, because he understands that it is unreasonable to expect first or second quartile results for all measures per function at any given time. He tells his people this, regularly.

John will also say that his monthly meetings provide him good information for stockholders and the Board of Directors and he is satisfied about how the process is working. He will add that he feels the process is motivating to his people throughout the organization. "I can walk the halls and see recognition of these data everywhere I go," he crows. "At every level, people understand what is expected of them!"

Below John, people spend hours coming up with explanations for their data compared to industry standard, and they do so with anxiety. "I cannot possibly reduce head count if we are also going to implement a new customer management system AND modify our output processes. No one seems to understand that this year we just won't make much progress on several key measures. I'm just going to look like I don't know what I'm doing!"

We can easily imagine the time and energy that is devoted to managing all the stories about the results, rather than being invested in producing real change that matters to the business. In fact, every month for several days people spend hours preparing for the monthly review meetings. That is, people are preparing for the meeting, not preparing to make the business better. They are spending precious resources to look good, smooth things over, or create erudite excuses that deflect attention from themselves, and if possible shift blame onto someone else or some other department when results do not look good.

So much of this has happened over the past year that there is very little conversation about meeting objectives. Each leader attends the appropriate monthly or quarterly meetings and reports on what has happened to date. Many make excuses for not meeting expectations and some say very little in an effort to avoid drawing more criticism than necessary.

It is not unusual for one leader to blame another for getting in the way or not providing needed information or resources. Each leader then either breathes a sigh of relief when it's over or heads for the bar to drink off the peripheral foul taste from licking various boots in an attempt to make amends. This is but a temporary respite as the after effects of shame linger, sometimes unseen, for a long time.

In a short period of time, John has led his organization into a climate of fear, where people are not at their best. While he genuinely believes his own story about the metrics and motivation, in fact John is sowing seeds of his own demise as his organization fails to accomplish important goals.

Changing Reality to Avoid Blame

Veronica is the head of human resources for a large consumer-products firm, and has been in the position for 17 years. During this time, she has seen many initiatives come and go. She has led some of them and she has resisted some of them. Veronica is seen as a thoughtful leader who uses critical thinking about complex issues to advise her peers and others.

Several years ago, Veronica resisted a request from the CEO to assess the talent of all leaders in Vice President or higher positions. The CEO prevailed and a consulting firm was brought in to provide information about bench strength at the executive level. Veronica stayed at arms length from the effort, delegating the entire process to managers lower in her organization.

The consultants conducted extensive assessments of these leaders, produced a report and presented their findings to the CEO and his direct reports. The data clearly indicated that, generally, executive talent in these key executives was not sufficient to take on the competition and that there was clear evidence that this "talent gap" in the leadership ranks was directly driving suboptimal performance in the marketplace.

The consultants reviewed the results with the executive team, talked about what could happen to improve the situation, and asked for additional time with various functional groups to begin helping people make good decisions about what to do.

Several executive team members, the President in particular, were alarmed by the report and wanted action immediately. The executive team put together a plan to communicate appropriate results and drive an action plan.

During the first month of action, Veronica began to challenge the reality of the message. Accepting the data meant that the lack of leadership talent was Veronica's fault. After all, as head of HR she was responsible for talent throughout the organization. For her, the contents of this report induced a feeling of blame that she was not willing to tolerate.

Within two months, Veronica had successfully convinced the majority of the executive team that the data were incorrect or unhelpful. After all, each of the executives had played a role in hiring and retaining the very employees who were now viewed suspiciously. They could avoid being on the receiving end of the blame game by either taking fast, decisive action (such as hiring additional talent, focusing on developing the current talent, and revving up their own coaching efforts for their people) or they could join Veronica in her campaign to sweep the situation under the rug.

By undermining the data and lobbying to reinterpret the message, Veronica successfully brought a halt to any activity that fit with a message that leadership could be improved in this organization. The organization continued on its steady course of deteriorating brand image and market share.

Veronica's behavior is a classic example of avoiding shame and blame.

Playing the Shame Game

Let us keep in mind that our ancestors protected the survival of the clan by practicing ostracism. In that era, complete ostracism nearly always led to death.   Each of us knows how bad it feels to be turned away. And yet it is a daily part of our existence, this feeling of shame and blame (ours or witnessing others').

Even if you could forage enough food to stay alive in Gur's time, being pushed out of the clan meant a seriously constrained environment.   Alone, defending oneself against the elements such as weather and predators became almost impossible.   In addition, if you didn't find another clan and receive acceptance, reproduction was out of the question, and the drive for this is biologically imperative.   So maintaining clan membership and status within the clan became critical at all costs.

Shame is a feeling we associate with events that get attached to us that lower our standing in the eyes of others. It threatens our ability, from a primitive perspective, to breed and feed. It reduces the quality of our lives. We are highly motivated when feeling shame to stop feeling it.   We work hard to avoid the feeling and consider shaming events extremely aversive. Shaming, in fact, is punishing. One of the principal ways we protect ourselves from shame is to blame others.

Blame is what we do to push lost opportunities onto others. By shifting a shaming event from ourselves to others and then creating distance from that person, we maintain our membership and status in the clan.

A sad but clear example of this can be found in the Magic Johnson story.   Magic Johnson was selected first overall in the 1979 NBA Draft and was Most Valuable Player in his rookie season. He was honored as one of the 50 Greatest Players in NBA history in 1996 and enshrined in the Basketball Hall of Fame in 2002.   In addition, he was beloved by his fans because of his kind nature and philanthropy.

In 1991, Magic Johnson retired abruptly after being diagnosed with HIV. Although he continued to play, his career was never the same. A hero in the eyes of many basketball fans and sports enthusiasts, Magic Johnson lost status within his "clan" (Western society) from a health diagnosis that people found frightening.

Immediately, people - many of them previously close to and admiring of the player - made decisions about how he acquired the disease, judged his behavior as shameful, and openly criticized him, which separated them from the shame and maintained their status in the clan. The ultimate message was: it is his fault he has HIV, I would never do what he did to get it, so I am different from him. Clear my name.

Over the years Mr. Johnson has worked, with some considerable success, to overcome this challenge. Yet, there is no question that his standing within his clan dropped and he has probably not regained a place he might have held had this episode not occurred.

Shame and blame are tremendously motivating. People will take swift and extreme action to avoid shame and blame others.

If we use shame or blame as a tool to influence others, fearful behaviors will follow. The long standing drive to avoid this kind of notoriety has such substantial potency that, as a leader, if you hold another up for public ridicule, you are practically ensuring the worst from that person in response. You are even reinforcing to others that shaming is possible, thereby indirectly ensuring the worst from them! Doing all this, by the way, means your old brain is engaging theirs.

The old brain, then, as the seat of emotion, becomes very active whenever even a hint of potential for shame wafts through the air. Your old brain has identified this threat long before you have even a faint conscious awareness of it.

On top of that, our western culture is very much a blaming one. People seldom have accidents any more. Someone must be at fault. An entire legal industry has blossomed around this process. Not only must someone be at fault, that fault needs to be made public so the appropriate shame can be dished out. Apparently it doesn't hurt if a little cash changes hands either.

In the workplace, we see this labeled as "CYA." When there is a problem, a lot of attention is placed on determining who is to blame. We will all work hard to make sure "it isn't me!"

It remains important to keep in mind that this process doesn't begin with a conscious decision to avoid responsibility. Our old brain fires up and begins nudging us in that direction in subtle but powerful ways.   Seldom does anyone say, even to themselves, "I'm going to lay this one on Joe and keep myself in the clear."   But our old brains can make it seem like the right thing to do, without even thinking about it.

What Can You Do?

Reducing, if not eliminating, the shame and blame game from your own repertoire is laudable, but it is exceedingly difficult. We often trigger reactions without knowing it.   However, here are some actions you can take to set yourself and others up for success.

- **Focus on Solutions**

    If shaming and blaming is happening, there is limited focus on what to actually do because the focus is on separating oneself from the person being blamed.   So getting focused on what can be done can pull people away from their fear.

    Ask yourself and others key questions to focus on finding a reasonable solution.

    - What improvement are you looking for?
    - How can you best get there?
    - What other options do you have?

    Moving into an analytical view of a better future can reduce the swirl of blame.

- **Ignore Calls for Blame and Accept Reality**

    Remember that people point the blame at others to keep from having any shame splatter on them. If you ignore their calls for blame and focus on moving forward, you are helping them see that there is no shaming to be experienced by anyone. Everyone makes mistakes, everyone does stupid stuff, and everyone lives to overcome it. Help people see and accept the reality of the situation as well as a path for moving forward safely.

- ## Let Go Of Your Grudges

We fall into the blaming trap more easily when we are holding grudges and resentments toward others. If you can work through any past issues so that you both understand how to move forward effectively, you have done yourselves and the organization a favor. If you cannot do this, then change your story about this individual so that your discomfort with the other person is controllable.

Tension between people is a normal part of life, and unless the tension is caused because one of you has a raised machete, you and your organization will benefit from allowing yourself and others to work through it, not get stuck within it.

- ## Follow the 10:1 Rule

People will feel less threatened by you personally if you have a "full" emotional bank account. It strengthens their status in the clan in ways that prevent one "withdrawal" from scaring them into blaming behavior.

- ## Avoid Asking Why

There are many ways to reach an understanding of any given event or situation without using the "why" word. This word has the ability to sound shameful regardless of tone or timber. "Give me some background on this" or "Help me understand what happened" can work better in gathering information, and it may keep you from slipping into a blame posture.

A significant problem with "why" questions is their historical focus. They look back instead of looking forward. They beg the respondent to come up with excuses for past behavior rather than focus on ways to be successful in the future.

Everything you can do to improve yourself or your circumstances lies in the future.

A more effective approach is something like: "If you were to face this situation again, what things could you do to ensure success? ...... Okay, those are good ideas. ..... Here is another idea you can consider. ...... What do you think is the best course of action?"

- ## Believe in Your Own Survival

The more threatened you feel, the less likely you will be able to rein in your own blaming. The truth is, you are unlikely to die as a result of your mistake. You probably won't even be bruised.

In most organizations, people who separate out the emotional agony of making mistakes from the business impact of those mistakes typically fare well. One of the best ways to accomplish this is to share the situation with someone you trust. An outside perspective is often more realistic than our own.

- ## Take a Time Out

Resist the temptation to take immediate action once you have learned of someone's mistake, including your own. Go for a cup of coffee, take a walk, or find some other activity that gives you personal space to allow your old brain to calm down a bit. Once you have soothed your old brain a bit, you can begin rebuilding your story about the situation in a way that is more effective for you and the organization. Once you have learned to buffer yourself from shame, your people are more likely to feel safe as well.

• Use Metrics for Data, not for Management

All metrics are provided after-the-fact. Data are dead. You cannot breathe life into them! Use them, then, as a way of imagining a better future, not as a way of managing people's behavior. The critical question is not, why are the data this way, although it may be helpful to understand how the data are gathered and calculated. Rather, the better approach is, "What are the data telling us? What can we do now to move forward, get better, be more successful?"

In our experience, a significant portion of data reviewed in business is not actionable or helpful. So, for example, a monthly budget review meeting that goes over line items is only helpful if looking at each line item leads to a decision to do or not do something in the future. Examine your own meetings and ask your people what they are doing differently as a result of the data review.

• Public Applause, Private Appeals

It is great to call out success in a group setting (although some people who are more reserved might consider it rather aversive!)

Nothing is more shaming, however, than being singled out in front of others for any kind of appeal for improvement. If you cannot avoid it, use tentative, future oriented language so people understand that you are striving for future success, not assigning blame for past failure.

Reducing feelings of shame and efforts to blame in your own actions and in your environment will pay huge dividends in people's ability to think creatively, solve difficult problems, and drive for results.

7.
The Trouble Meter

Because we have a tendency to zero in on what is wrong, as we have touched on several times already, it is often helpful to notice people's reactions to know how much trouble we are getting ourselves into!   Unfortunately, there is no one set of criteria for correctly determining what people's reactions are around us. But there are some general rules.   In fact, you have already known about them for a long time.   This is the foundation for what we call the Trouble Meter.

People vary in their ability to do so, but we all pick up the emotional vibrations of others.   Quick or sudden movements get most people's attention.   Many of us will interpret tone changes or verbal expletives as danger signals.   Some pick up subtleties such as eye movements and pauses in speech as reason for concern.   We all possess that strong and basic ability to sense danger from the reactions of others in our immediate vicinity.

In the business place of today, we become accustomed to the standard emotional range of others and adapt. This is part of our "automated" processing activity that goes on in the background. Someone who is calm on a regular basis will catch our attention more quickly with a raised voice or startled response. Similarly, if someone yells all the time, we tend to pay little attention to the yelling. Remember the story of the boy who cried wolf? We all tend to respond the way his village did.

At issue in being our best is noticing when our own old brain resonance is raised because of someone else's old brain behavior. If someone yells at you, your old brain will likely respond, and you could find yourself yelling back in no time. It may feel good and right, but if you review times when you have been involved in a yell-fest, you may find that nothing worthwhile really happened. Often, in fact, we have to return to the "scene of the crime" and do a little backfilling to sustain an acceptable working relationship.

Toxic Fumes

Katherine is the managing partner of a large services firm. During a growth period, she hired several experienced professionals in her firm. One, Jason, came with considerable experience and hit the ground running. Katherine was pleased and gave Jason all the support she could to enable his success.

Slowly, Katherine began to hear carefully worded concerns about Jason. She also began to hear more bickering and complaining in general around the office. Her initial reaction was confusion, so she began to ask for more information. The stories she was hearing were at odds with her experiences of Jason. People were not very forthcoming in response to her requests. This continued for awhile, although at partner meetings, the subject of "poor morale" increased, and these stories and Jason's success began to intertwine.

Katherine had several conversations with Jason to find out how he felt things were going and what his perspective was about the firm and its people. Jason wove a story that sounded positive and seemed credible in the moment. On reflection, though, Katherine found the conversations to contain little of real substance. She began to feel that Jason never really said much, although he talked a lot! At last, her tolerance for continuing in this vague situation dropped to zero, and she asked for help.

During a set of interviews with Jason and other employees, it was discovered that Jason was disruptive in very subtle yet very powerful ways. He did not like to follow some of the procedures of the firm. These procedures were different from what he was accustomed to in his previous positions - more focused on teamwork, process efficiency, and a specific client focus. Following these procedures, he felt, caused more work for him. Not following them caused more work for others. When others complained, he began to argue his case for doing it his way. His stories showcased his knowledge and experience in ways both subtle and not so subtle, while seriously undermining well grounded, effective processes that were at the heart of this firm's success.

Most insidious was how he construed himself as a victim. Through coffee room gossiping, Jason was able to recruit a stable of younger associates as his acolytes. They then began to pass around stories about how Jason was being singled out and picked on. A seriously negative swirl began to attend his every move.

Because Jason made it a point to be friendly and helpful to his acolytes, those upon whose backs his work fell began to complain. His followers came to his defense, of course, and people began to bicker. What had been a cohesive professional firm became a beehive of blame and defensiveness.

Jason was what is sometimes called a "toxic" employee. He was very technically skilled, he was very good with his clients, and he was interpersonally very likable. However, Jason did not fit into this organization very well because of his resistance to standardized work processes and a collaborative approach, and this poor fit began to work the same way as pouring ammonia and bleach into the same container - the combination was noxious and dangerous.

The fumes from this noxious combination wafted into Katherine's space in such small doses that she was at first unable to identify the source.

Once the poor fit issues were identified, Katherine and Jason were able to have concrete and helpful discussions about how to make things work.   Eventually, Jason decided to leave with Katherine's help and blessing.   The organization immediately began to shift back to a more effective workplace.

Sharing The Pain

Charlie is a level headed and solid leader in a large banking institution.   Most would describe him as fun,   interesting, experienced in his field and good at sound problem solving. Most who knew him would also describe Charlie as "moody." When Charlie is happy, you know it.   When Charlie is not happy, you know it.

A common situation with Charlie is how he handles passing in-formation on to his people upon returning from higher level meetings. He feels it is very important to keep people informed, so he has weekly meetings and passes on information from

other parts of the organization. When he attends a meeting in which there is information to pass on, he often calls a "standing meeting" as soon as he returns. By this, he means that people gather somewhere - the conference room, the hallway - and stand together, rather than sit, for a few minutes while he shares information.

Charlie often comes back from higher level meetings frustrated. People see him coming and a general "uh-oh" feeling infuses the office. By the time people meet him in the conference room, there is a high-level resonance of energy and stress. Before Charlie even opens his mouth, people are worried about what they will hear. Often, Charlie's first words will not even be heard, because the stress level has everyone preoccupied with their own safety.

Even when Charlie does not share bad news but simply provides updates, people will go away asking themselves and each other, "What did I miss?" and "What will happen now?" Without intending to, Charlie has transferred his own old brain agitation to his team under the guise of "communicating."

If this happened once or twice, it would not have much impact on the organization. But because Charlie is seen as a barometer for danger in the workplace, people's trouble meters drive them to spend significant time and energy watching him instead of doing work. In addition, his distracting impact has people's old brains vibrating in lieu of doing the sound analytical work required. Charlie's organizational unit has a long way to go to be its most effective.

Brain Resonance

Your old brain is extremely resonant to old brain activity in those around you. There was significant evolutionary advantage to being able to sense emotional arousal in others. If you were good at this, you could evacuate before a situation became seriously threatening. As you and a primitive colleague foraged in a forest, a startled response from your pal would likely, and helpfully, startle you as well. And if he tore off in a run without pointing or communicating with you, you were best served by doing the same. If you weren't good at this, you were more likely to be severely thrashed by an agitated colleague or fall prey to other danger.   Any ancient ancestors who weren't good at this kind of resonant response didn't get to be our ancestors after all.

"There was a time when one degree was enough, but now you'll be competing against younger people with degrees in both hunting and gathering."

All of our senses are attuned at many levels to the emotional state of those around us.   If you walk into an office and two people there have been arguing, you can feel it as you enter the room.   You may not know the source of the agitation, but you certainly know there is some. Most of us have learned to pay attention to the "prickle" on the back of our neck, even if we don't immediately know why.

Not only are we *aware* of the agitation in others, but we tend to *respond* with an increased level of agitation ourselves. In most cases, we experience this agitation before we are aware of it. It makes sense, even today, that if the individual next to you is scared, it may be a good idea to be scared yourself, even before you know what the other person is scared of. As we saw with our ancestor in the forest, you would bolt then, and so you bolt now, although the "bolting" is less obvious.

All of our senses are attuned at many levels to the emotional state of those around us.

In the current business world, if you get the sense that your boss is upset, your old brain will kick in. If you sense agitation in others, you are likely to feel some agitation. If someone else is yelling, you may feel like yelling back (or fleeing or freezing). If others are cynical and critical, you may begin to feel that way as well. Unfortunately, when we are agitated and old-brain driven, our plans tend to be vague and our decisions are impulsive and simplistic. We are not bringing the best of ourselves to the table.

"Our plan has two parts. First, we make our first sale. Next, we dominate the market."

Kipling, a very astute observer of the human condition, wrote that it is no easy feat to keep your head while those about you lose theirs. There may even be some contemporary value for your old brain to respond in this way – certainly, being able to read the emotional state of others allows us to investigate issues and help others be their best. Keep in mind, though, that when your old brain begins to hum in response to another's, you get all the other baggage of your old brain, often without being aware of it.

What Can You Do?

We are fortunate to have a trouble meter to alert us to danger. Remember, though, that our old brain is over adapted for today's environment, and it is helpful to be aware of our own responses to a jump in the meter. Here are some suggestions on how to do this.

- ### Take a Time Out

   When it is your old brain taking off in high stride, take a break. In Charlie's case, he could have gotten a lot of mileage out of taking a detour from his executive meetings to walk around the building, rather than proceed immediately to meet with his people. Once he cooled down, thought it through, or simply relaxed, his old brain could disengage enough for his standing meeting and his direct reports would not experience the overflow. At that point, he and his people could be more effective.

- ### Test Your Story

   Your old brain may be revving up for no reason. In fact, it probably is. Okay, the boss said "Cut your expenses by 10%" but what he really meant might have been "Times are rough, we've got some hard choices to make, give me your best recommendation."

   It is not necessary to ask your boss to confirm this new story. You can simply proceed as if it is true, if it helps you be more effective.

   A good question to ask yourself here is, "What else?" Push yourself to do a little more thinking about the message, the intent, the circumstances, etc.. instead of just reacting. As we know, this kind of thinking is new brain activity and that is where you will be at your best.

- ## Recognize Old Brain Energy and Give It a Break

  If you are sensing a highly charged emotional reaction, assume that the individual squirting all those fumes actually wants, more than anything, to be his or her best. Remember that when the old brain is running the show, we are all lacking the resources to think analytically and logically, see a positive future, and express ourselves clearly and effectively.

  By recognizing that someone is in an old brain rant, you can calm your own reaction by accepting that it is not about you, it is not what they really mean, and it is not them being at their best. Giving them this benefit of your doubt will allow you to be your best in the circumstance.

- ## Use Some Humor

  One of the truly important roles of humor is to discharge old brain activity in a less dangerous or harmful way. Laughter does lighten our load. Of course, be careful that the humor is not demeaning or hurtful to anyone.

- ## Postpone Critical Decisions

  It may feel right to take immediate action. However, in many cases, you and your business will be better served if you postpone action until you, and others, have calmed down.

  Think about the individual who is agitated and use one of the recommendations for action above. For some, postponing the meeting for 15-20 minutes, or even longer sometimes, might give them enough time to calm down and release their old brain energy. For others, you know you cannot postpone the meeting, so try another approach.

Be thoughtful about your reaction and pay attention to your own old brain energy. Take care of yourself.

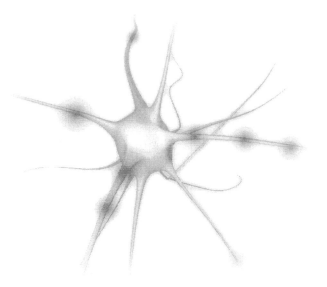

8.
Not in My House!

One of the more common challenges facing contemporary organizations across the country and the world is what is often referred to as "siloing." A silo in an organization often represents a functional area, where clear boundaries of responsibility have been delineated. These "silos" serve a necessary purpose of clarifying who will do what and allowing responsible individuals to be held accountable to get certain work done.

"Siloing" as a label, however, tends to have a negative connotation. When you are accused of siloing, it means that you are focusing on your part of the organization to the detriment of others. In a word, you are behaving *territorially*.

"Simmons, it's been brought to my attention that you've been trying to grab Filbert's carrot."

The confusion between setting helpful boundaries and behaving territorially is fundamental to many, many organizational problems.   Functional organizations often struggle with cooperation, collaboration, creative thinking, and decision making.   Matrix organizations often struggle with these as well as with outright undermining efforts.   What we seldom discuss or even recognize is that our territorial imperative is part of our old brain's way of protecting us and helping us survive.   And yes, you guessed it.   Once again our old brain is over adapted for today's world.

I've Got Mine, You Take Care of Yours

Kevin's story is a common one.   As a member of the leadership team at a large production plant, he was recognized as having great ideas about how to reduce costs and increase efficiencies. His group's function within the plant was maintaining all the equipment, facilities and buildings.   The plant had a regular preventive maintenance program when Kevin entered his role, but they suffered with effectively scheduling and maintaining equipment that went offline unexpectedly.

One of the reasons for this was that the people who operated the equipment had come to expect immediate gratification.   The argument was a good one: if the equipment isn't working properly, it is keeping people from being productive, and therefore the plant is losing money.   This story had led to the maintenance function taking on a "get it fixed now" mentality, which of course led to the expectation of immediate gratification on the part of those in the operations function. With unlimited resources, this would have worked.   However, when there is only so much to go around in terms of human, capital and time resources, people are bound to be disappointed and frustrated.

To combat this very real concern, Kevin issued the "Rules of Maintenance."   A process for requesting work was put in place.

He decided who should be involved at what level depending upon the criticality of the request. A standing set of meetings was put in place. As each stage of the process was implemented, he would get approval of the executive team. Often, the team would approve his plans with caveats: he could implement these changes as long as he understood that issues never resolved themselves this easily, and collaboration would be required.

Kevin was very territorial in his approach. His colleague in charge of the operations function, Harvey, was very collaborative. Over time, their conversations began to take on a certain pattern. Harvey would go to Kevin to work out an issue. Kevin would cite the Rules of Maintenance. Harvey would try to discuss with Kevin how the rules weren't working. Kevin would cite the Rules of Maintenance. Harvey would go away frustrated and drive himself crazy trying to think of another approach to Kevin that would generate flexibility for the immediate circumstance. Kevin would get over the conversation quickly. After all, he was taking care of his business, which was maintenance of the plant. Harvey would just have to take care of the operations of the plant.

Kevin's overall thinking was sound and his processes were good processes. His rigid approach to only worrying about his function, however, led to frustration and anger. Over time, the operators and the maintenance workers were at each other's throats. Managers in the two functions were yelling at each other. Harvey was working with his people to help them cooperate, so he was losing credibility! And Kevin was blind to the havoc he was wreaking.

It's What I Get Paid to Do

There are some organizational processes that actually foment territorialism, and pay programs fall squarely into this category. Here is a story about how that frequently works negatively for an organization and its people.

A large consulting firm established lucrative incentive programs
for its regional vice presidents.   Each RVP had a clear set of
boundaries about which offices in which countries fell within
his or her region.   The issue arose regularly, however, that work
being performed for a specific client would be spread across
regions.   This meant that a consultant in one office could be
responsible for the client relationship and yet dependent upon a
consultant in an office across the state, country, or even around
the world to actually do the work.

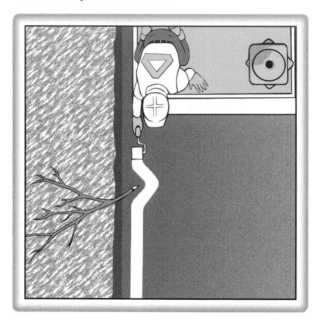

Because the consultants were well trained and good at their
jobs, they would sometimes disagree about what the right thing
to do with this client might be, given geographic and cultural
differences.   Because the consultants were working long hours
for many different clients, sometimes they put more effort into
the client they understood best, and did a less diligent job for a
client they didn't understand well because another consultant
was responsible for maintaining that relationship.   So, due to
these very real and difficult geographic and client issues, battles
would ensue.

Martin and Jennifer, two of these RVPs, regularly got into serious arguments about who would "get credit" for both the sale of the work as well as the work production itself. Both of them were clear: there was one primary reason that these arguments took place. "My pay is on the line here," Jennifer explained. "Don't set me up with a big potential payout and then expect me to play nice!"

Martin had the same perspective. "I give in on this one with the understanding that I get to win the next one. I hope Jennifer gets her full payout. But not at my expense!"

"I can't afford to give both of you a raise. You'll have to settle it with a cage fight."

The distorted compensation system led both these key executives to completely lose sight of their responsibilities - to their clients, to their employees, to the company's mission. Their need to protect their territory had taken front and center stage. It's understandable, but still not an example of people doing their best work.

Our Limited Territorial View

Many animals acquire and defend territory, and our ancestors were no exception. It was clearly to the advantage of early humans to protect good hunting and gathering territory. The drive to feed and breed was fundamental to survival, so an initial reinforcer to the continuation of the species was to protect these opportunities.

If another clan entered Gur's territory, it was critical that Gur and his clan take action to reduce the new clan's impact. The new clan could not be allowed to reduce the harvest in any way, and they could not be allowed to infiltrate the clan in search of procreation opportunities. There were exceptions to this. One obvious exception was survival - if Gur's clan had for any reason - disease, famine, hurricane - been reduced in number to a threatening level, allowing the merging of another clan would increase its ranks effectively.

But a key action on the part of any human was and is to protect identified territory. This plays out today as well – someone cuts in front of us in traffic, and we may have a territorial single-digit response.

Our need to protect our territory plays out in many ways. Obviously, we have a physical territory that we protect. In the United States, it is a common understanding that you can protect your home from a burglar, including the use of deadly force. In other words, my home is worth more than your life. This is the very most basic territorial protection at work. It is hard to imagine that we would ever have come up with this cultural view if we did not first have a territory protecting imperative built into our DNA.

We defend our
psychological territory.

We also see our responsibilities as our territory. We are responsible for our children and are protective of them above all else. If we feel our children are threatened, we become extremely focused in expunging the threat.

We are also responsible for our own behavior, and therefore become defensive when criticized. We have job responsibilities and become territorial there.

In addition, in contemporary humans, territoriality is not just about "Don't come into my yard," but also about "Don't tell me what I can think or feel." We are motivated to defend our psychological space. When an attempt is made to directly influence what we think or feel – especially what we feel – our natural territorial response from our old brain is to resist and defend. We all do this, and most of the time we do it without thinking about it. If our old brain interprets that we are threatened, even if it is the threat of an idea that we don't like, we will respond with old brain overtones, if not overt old brain behavior. And, remember, we are not making a choice or decision to be defensive. The defensive behavior happens before we are aware of it.

Imperative language is an intrusion on the psychological territory of others.

In the workplace, we see this when we think someone else is being "defensive." Often, that is exactly what is happening – they are, indeed, *defending themselves from a threat*. Their old brain has sensed something in the interaction that leads them to defend themselves.

If we examine these interactions, we often see there is an attempt to "invade the territory" of the subject. A common example is when we tell someone what he or she "needs" or "has" to do. Actually, the list of things that we really need or have to do is quite small and generally limited to things like breathing. Most of life is optional, especially at work.

This is not to say that the consequences can't or won't be unpleasant. And unpleasant consequences may result in our feeling we really have no options, but that is just self-deception. A simple example is this: you can choose to work whatever hours you wish. The consequences vary depending upon your choices. If you choose to work long hours, the consequences could turn out to be a raise or promotion. If you choose to work irregular, unpredictable hours, the consequences may turn out to be an opportunity to find another job.

Focus on behavior, not attitude.

Keeping in mind the simplistic nature of the old brain, it is easy to imagine how telling someone that he/she "has to show up on time" can trigger a defense against the intrusion into personal psychological space. A more common example is when we attempt to "manage" an employee's attitude. An attempt to directly manage attitude in another is a clear invitation to an old brain tussle. Any parent of an adolescent can instantly sense the truth of this!

Unfortunately, once the interaction has escalated to a defensive level, it is not easy to resolve it in a positive way because our old brain will want to wrestle with the other person's old brain. Another person's defensiveness will elicit old brain activation in us. Let's call this the "old brain tango" – a passionate dance with an unhappy ending on many occasions. This also represents another version of old brain resonance.

What Can You Do?

Here are some actions you can take to reduce resistance, lower boundaries and eliminate "silo" thinking.

• Use Tentative Language

Language that limits people's choices - what we call imperative language - can trigger a territorial "get out of my business" response. When talking with someone about changing their approach or behavior, telling them they "have to" is a recipe for failure.

In Kevin's case, no one could tell him to do anything differently. The team would approve his Rules of Maintenance actions with the directive to "be collaborative" which was the equivalent of telling him to do it his way.

Harvey's efforts to engage Kevin in discussion were fraught with "you have to" and "we need to" language, so Kevin invoked his Rules. It may not be the answer to overcoming territorial responses, but tentative language can lead to a real discussion about options and consequences that others can understand and react to from their new brain.

• Focus on What Really Matters

Kevin suffered from "silo" thinking because he lost sight of what the plant was there to do. He clearly viewed his responsibilities as "maintenance only" which had no responsibility for the effective operation of the plant, the welfare of its people, or the ultimate customer's experience in terms of product or price. He was doing *his* job. Helping him focus on what really mattered would have been difficult, no question. It would take time and patience. This is part of great leadership, however: coaching people to be their best.

Kevin's boss, Alexander, regularly missed opportunities to reinforce better behavior for better results. Alexander could have created a competing story for Kevin and helped him learn to work within the new story.

Thinking through what he wanted to see from Kevin, Alexander could then begin to coach him regularly. The new story could have sounded like this: "Your Rules of Maintenance seem to be well founded for your staff in maintenance. I do not see, however, how can we expect the overall plant to work effectively if we do not have rules that work for everyone, and your rules are focused exclusively on maintenance. We will spend as much time as it takes to work out how to incorporate your rules, Kevin, into the overall working of the plant, and we will get Harvey and his operations people involved in coming up with an overall process that works. I want to be involved regularly, so I can see how progress is being made and the impact it is having."

Alexander could then take advantage of positively reinforcing the boundary spanning activities as they happened.

Unfortunately, Alexander thought he was having an impact by dictating to Kevin what he wanted. He imagined that Kevin would hear it, understand it, and do it. It seldom works this way.

• Focus on What Really Matters, Again

This is fodder for another complete book, but putting incentive pay in competition with what really matters is bad business. We are all living the results of this approach right now, in the form of bank failures and Wall Street greed.

If you are in a position to rethink your pay plans, do so. If not, focus on reinforcing what is right and solve the incentive dilemma in other ways. If you hear someone use their personal incentive payout potential as an excuse for doing the wrong thing, set an expectation that talking in this way is not helpful. Take advantage of the opportunity to talk about the bigger picture.

Jacqueline, a sales person, was overheard by her boss, Peter, telling a colleague, Scott, that she was not going to receive her commission if Scott did not take specific action immediately. Peter called her into his office right then and challenged Jacqueline to imagine why Scott would care if Jacqueline received her commission. "But a long term and loyal customer is waiting for product right now," Jacqueline squealed. Peter responded, "Now there, Jacqueline, is the reason Scott should take action!"

Talent is always conscious of its own abundance, and does not object to sharing. --Alexander Solzhenitsyn

---

People will show up every day and work hard for money, although they may not do the right things for the business. People will do great work with energy, creativity and enthusiasm for a great cause. What is the great mission of your organization? Who in your company really knows it? Who can you point to who really internalizes it?

- ## Take Advantage of the Emotional Bank Account

Territorial defensiveness is triggered by a threat to enter a territory uninvited or for reasons that are unclear or that exceed available resources. Each of these territorial "incursion" is a withdrawal from the Emotional Bank Account you have with the other person. If you have made enough deposits, you can make a withdrawal with little consequence. This is an area, however, where withdrawals are large and therefore dry up the account quickly, so be prepared to pay a lot of attention to the outstanding balance.

• Redefine the Boundaries

Find ways to remind people that they are on the same team. Eliminate as many reminders as possible that people are working in separate units. Avoid putting different units in competition. Let us remember that competition by its very nature is about winning and losing. You want everyone to win in their endeavors.

"This issue is very complex and has troubling implications. It involves me letting go of turf."

Talk about how you see boundaries being crossed in effective ways and encourage others to talk about their successes as well. Alexander could have gotten some serious mileage at his plant by regularly saying things like "Harvey has been working daily with Kevin to work out how Kevin's Rules of Maintenance can be incorporated effectively into the Operations Function. It is this collaboration between these two that demonstrate how we can serve our employees and our business most effectively. I look forward to seeing more of this type of behavior from everyone."

Boundaries are helpful only when everyone agrees on what they are and how they work. If my boundary is your frustration, additional discussion and problem solving can make a real difference.

• Challenge Others To Make Their Business Case

Establish a clear expectation that as part of the debate, participants make their case for your customers, or excellence, or cost reduction, or whatever you define as key drivers of your true business pursuit. Interrupt the "I" and "me" language so prevalent in these kinds of disputes and reframe the discussion in terms of the grand pursuit of the business and relentlessly insist that others do the same.

• Facilitate an Intentional Leadership Discussion

Remember that whether it is in an individual, one-on-one interaction or within a larger group meeting, the intentional leadership discussion includes four elements that move you, your people and your organization forward.

> *What is the goal?* Let's remember, every chance we get, why we are here and what really matters. It is too easy to become distracted by very real, very compelling issues that simply are not helpful in getting us to our desired results. If we continue to talk about this every chance we get, we are more likely to keep on track.

> *What behavior are we talking about?* Given a specific territorial defense, for example, what do we want to see happen? What behavior, no matter how difficult, will move us forward rather than pin us down in a foxhole of our own making?

> *What positive consequences will result from this behavior?* Let us be specific about this, because it may well be the negative consequences that people fear that have them behaving territorially. What good comes

from behaving differently, as we identified and described above?

What commitment are we willing to make? Once we've talked all this through, what will people step up and promise to make happen? Public commitments help us do what we say we are going to do, and everyone benefits from the repetitive and predictable keeping of commitments.

We will always have these tendencies toward territorial thinking, but it does not mean we cannot overcome them. Siloing can be reduced!

9.
I Want It All and I Want It Now!

One of the strongest drives we experience in our lifetimes is a drive to take care of our own needs. This drive comes from our DNA and is focused on us getting what we want at a very basic level. We do not have to worry about this drive being diminished or ignored; we are always going to take care of our own needs in some way.

How has this drive played out in our businesses and leadership? Not always optimally. Our powerful drive to take care of "me" will often play out in pushing a personal agenda, manipulating others, and even justifying criminal or unethical behavior. This often feels okay to us because our story is that we feel this way on behalf of the business. But others see through this false front to the real personal drivers behind "me"-based leadership.

We have socialized this drive in our society in interesting ways. It is okay to "win" in business, put someone else out of business, trick our customers into paying more than something is worth, and generally take advantage of others, all in the name of Good Business. The recent meltdown in our economy clearly has its roots here. This is a manifestation of one of our basest drives. Most of us hope that we can do better than this, as individuals and as leaders.

Buy It and Fix It

Several years ago, a large company purchased a new plant for a good price because the plant itself was old, with a good deal of "deferred maintenance," and was not producing profitably. The executive team immediately relieved the plant leadership team of its responsibilities and sent in its own group of people from various of its other locations to run the plant. This new group of leaders was given a very specific mandate: fix it.

George, the new plant manager, did not have a say in who his new direct reports on his new team would be - six new managers converged upon this plant in about a two-month period. George had a reputation of pulling together troubled plants, and all of his new directors had reputations of "getting things done." George immediately set them free to, well, get it done.

You probably know people like these managers. With a history of fixing things and turning around a business unit, they know what needs to get done. What else would these managers do but get down to the task of telling their teams what needed to be done? This is okay in theory, but in practice it can be quite ineffective. A couple of quick   examples of comments made with one of their teams will serve to illustrate the fatal flaw of these leaders' approach.

> "Listen up, guys! Here is what I want you to do............"

> "I don't want to hear any excuses. This gets done on today's shift or you have me to answer to."

Surely you have heard similar language at some point in your career. It feels powerful to the speaker. It is, but in the wrong way. The selfish immediacy is clearly perceived by anyone present.

This same selfish immediacy began to play itself out in the leadership team as well. Conversations in the leadership team meetings began to sound like:

> Manager A: "I need to move three contract engineers to Unit 3 or I won't meet my deadline."

> Manager B: "No! I need those engineers or I won't meet my deadline."

> George: "Do what you have to do, but I these expect deadlines to be met!"

Whether any one of these managers was ultimately right or wrong really doesn't matter. The selfish immediacy of their old brains kept them from getting the results that were critical for the business.

The impact on people in the plant was obvious and predictable. People felt they had no say in what was happening. They began to feel unappreciated, and resentment built toward their new leaders. Although they had been a group of employees who cared deeply about their work and their plant, over time they lost their concern for success, and many began to look elsewhere for work. Morale fell like a brick and regular and frequent breakdowns and shutdowns began to happen.

In the end, nobody was happy. The plant improvements were not happening on schedule. There were grumblings at every level in the employee pool. Corporate executives were disappointed in plant performance. The leadership team was broken up and moved to other positions. The plant was finally shut down for an extended period, and at enormous expense.

The Disappointment Cycle

Shirley was a leader in a mid-sized insurance company who was known for her passion and commitment to the firm. People were happy with Shirley, and she was viewed as a good leader. Behind closed doors, however, Shirley complained of being "constantly disappointed" by her staff. "They just don't seem to really care about the business," she lamented. "They do what I ask them to do, and they do it well, but it leaves me feeling like I have to think of all the answers *and* all the questions!"

It turned out that Shirley had created this situation for herself. When Shirley gets an assignment, or sees something that needs to be done, it becomes personal to her. "My reputation is on the line here." So she communicates in personal terms to her employees.

> "I know you are really busy, but I need for you to get this done for me."

> "I understand that you have other commitments, and they are all important. I want you to focus on these things first."

By communicating to her staff that their work is all about making her happy, Shirley is setting herself up for disappointment. Once she asks someone to take action on her behalf, if they don't do it, it will feel personal to Shirley. If they don't do a very good job of it, it will feel personal. If they don't demonstrate the same level of passion and excitement about it as she feels, it will feel personal.

How can others demonstrate the same level of passion? Who can get passionate about making their boss happy? Doing great work that is helpful or creative or delighting customers can generate passion. As an overarching goal, pleasing your boss is woefully inadequate. It is a recipe for drudgery.

These kinds of shortfalls often left Shirley feeling disappointed. It was not unusual for her to return to the employee and ask them "why" questions.

> "Why are you working on that assignment now? Do you think the other assignment I asked you to do will get done on time?"

> "Why do you think I asked you to do this now?"

It's unlikely that Shirley will ever feel very happy with her people. How can they live up to her expectations, when those expectations are about Shirley herself? Shirley's people weren't feeling very satisfied with their work and were not performing at their best. Overall, there was an opportunity for doing better business here.

Survive and Thrive Equals Immediate and Selfish

Even though the old brain does not have language, if it did, an internal dialogue might sound like "Me! Me! Now! Me! Now! Now! Me!"

Because the old brain has no future and the past runs together, everything takes on a *now* view. There is an impulsive drive for immediate closure, resolution, satisfaction, or safety.

In a primitive world, there was no reward for delaying reactions to threats.

This makes perfect sense given the evolutionary imperative for individual survival. The growl in the bushes is best served by an *immediate* response. Gathering food for the next meal made more sense than leaving food for another day. There was very little in the environment that reinforced an inclination to wait.

Those inclined to be patient and deliberative probably didn't get to be our ancestors.

The old brain is also disinclined to be primarily concerned with the personal welfare of others when danger lurks.   Our evolutionary imperative was first to ensure our own genes were propagated.   It did our individual DNA little good when we invested in the survival of others at our own expense. So we are selfish by nature.

Survival in Gur's time was clearly defined: feed and breed. Those who did not do both are not part of our DNA today. There was no payoff for taking care of anyone else until you had taken care of yourself. Any attention paid to offspring was driven by the same DNA, as part of the drive for reproduction.

The focus on ourselves connects directly to our survival. Like both the orientation to and response to threat, this is a powerful process that serves us well under extreme circumstances.

In a primitive environment, this will get you what you want, but it surely is not a recipe for effective leadership, teamwork or business behavior in general.   Often in the workplace, as expertly demonstrated by Shirley, this will be manifested with a lot of "I" language.   Issues are phrased in terms of what "I" want, what "I" need, or how soon "I" need it. Although there is a critical place for "I" language in the business world, it is not tied to outcomes but rather to clarifying the source of opinions, concerns and reactions.   Focusing on individual needs in business often leads to an escalating cycle of old brain agitation.

As in Shirley's case, here is how this cycle often plays out.

First, we are disappointed that we aren't getting what we want - an employee has failed to deliver as we desired. As our old brain agitation increases, the salience of the individual need is heightened. That is, we want what we want *more*. This engenders even more old brain activity. Others typically react to our elevated old brain activity with increased old brain activity of their own. The defensiveness of their old brain generates even more old brain activity on our part. And so it goes, on and on. This is a death spiral we all recognize, yet leave unchecked.

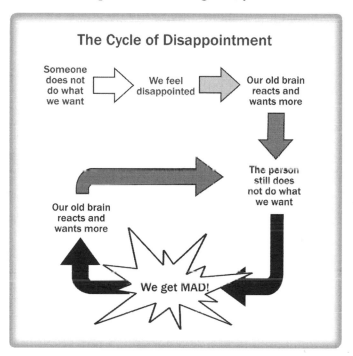

What Can You Do?

When our old brain is triggered, we might as well be screaming "I want it All! I want it Now! I want it to be Easy!!!" If it were ever true that it worked this way, of course, then our old brain would not be triggered in the first place. Here are some things you can do to overcome this old brain drive for selfishness in your own or others' experiences.

- ## Use Tentative Language

  Remember that imperative language shuts down options for people, and use language that allows a choice. This will reduce old brain responses. We are much less likely to respond with a demand for self-focus if we are given a choice to do things our way.

- ## Use the 10:1 Rule Authentically

  It is not uncommon to find ourselves making personal appeals or demands because of stress and worry that we have not reined in. If we have filled the Emotional Bank Account with enough deposits, people are more likely to respond helpfully. Shirley, however, shows us how not all deposits are the same.

  Shirley regularly gave her people "feel good" deposits. People knew she cared about them, and believed she wanted them to be successful. Her deposits were not always authentic, however, because she was actually quite disappointed with people. This backfired on her more than others, although given enough time, people began to feel unconnected to the business, which served no one.

- ## Separate Business From Personal

  If you have tied people's success to pleasing you, there is a high likelihood that you are regularly disappointed. People are there to do the work because the business you are in requires it. Tie their efforts to the business and its success, and they are less likely to engage your old brain in the cycle of disappointment.

- ## Avoid Singular Pronouns

  If you hear yourself overemphasizing what *you* want, usually manifested in "I" language, or if you find yourself feeling like "I never get what I want!" you may be identifying your own old brain selfish immediacy.

  Ask yourself how to talk about what matters without talking about yourself. "I want this now" probably means that you are feeling pressure to perform or are worried about how others see you. Is what you want really important to the success of the business? Can you communicate it in terms of how your customer or other stakeholders will benefit? Can you link the outcome to the larger vision of the business? If not, you may be falling prey to your own evolutionary drivers to take care of yourself.

• Challenge Your Own Stories

If you are in the throes of an old brain immediate need, ask yourself how realistic your story is, and how helpful it is. Remind yourself of the big picture and what really matters. Both the selfish (I want it!) and immediate (Now!) parts of our nature close down options for moving forward. Expand them! Ask yourself what else can be done to make this work well? If this were working well, what would I do next?

• Have an Intentional Leadership Conversation with Yourself

Recalling that the intentional leadership conversation has four questions, think about this:

- The first question in an intentional leadership conversation process is "What really matters here?" "I want it" is not a good answer! Remind yourself what really matters.

- Think about what it will take in terms of your own, personal behavior to get to what really matters.

- Think about the positive consequences of doing something differently, no matter how uncomfortable it makes you feel.

- Then, make a commitment to yourself to do it differently. Keeping a promise to yourself is a great first start in helping others keep their promises.

- **Take a Time Out**

  Whether it is you or someone else who is in the "Me! Now!" cycle, see if you can postpone the conversation to give the old brain a chance to simmer down. Setting a specific future time and date for the conversation will help you and the other person settle down more easily, knowing that there will still be an opportunity to discuss and resolve any issues.

- **Listen, Actively**

  Active listening is paying close attention with an intention of demonstrating that you care. When someone's old brain is active, they have put out their viewpoint of the moment and have run into resistance. A few moments of active listening can demonstrate that you heard their message and that they are entitled to their own thoughts and feelings. This will help the old brain energy recede.

  An old adage says, "People don't care how much you know until they know how much you care." Responding with empathic language provides a safe connection with emotional content, without your having to agree or condone.

  ## People don't care how much you know until they know how much you care.
  ## -- Unknown

- **Translate It to the Business**

  When someone is insisting on immediate action or putting their story forward first, respectfully juxtapose what they want with what really matters. "I understand that you want this to happen, and I'm struggling to understand how that helps us delight our customers." Use questions to move to a bigger, future picture. "What do you imagine will happen next? After that?" Getting ourselves and others to think out a realistic and desired future often helps calm old brain agitation.

Tap the "easy" button if you can, but otherwise these actions may help you and others get better results.

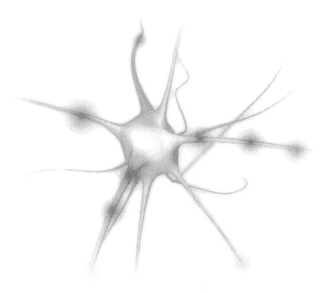

10.
The Seduction of
Simplicity

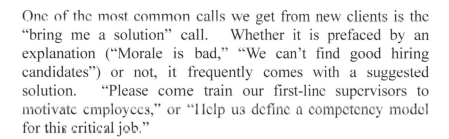

One of the most common calls we get from new clients is the "bring me a solution" call. Whether it is prefaced by an explanation ("Morale is bad," "We can't find good hiring candidates") or not, it frequently comes with a suggested solution. "Please come train our first-line supervisors to motivate employees," or "Help us define a competency model for this critical job."

Obviously, long before the call, these leaders have been dealing with problems that feel complex and difficult, and they call us when they feel they have tried to make a difference but are unsatisfied with it. This is a subtle explanation for how we get into old brain processing. Our old brain might as well be screaming at us: "I want it all! I want it now! I want it to be easy!"

Poor morale is rarely about one thing. One big clue about old brain energy is the simplicity of the solutions offered. It is undoubtedly true that first-line supervisors can benefit from leadership training, but this is only one small piece of the story.

This simplistic, one-dimensional solution traps this leader into dealing with poor morale with a superficial, off-target fix, when, in actuality, many people and processes are in play here.

"If You'd Just..." Leadership

Andrew is the head of all administrative functions at a large financial services institution.   He drives his people crazy because of his approach to getting things done.   Andrew is actually very good at setting clear goals, but he doesn't leave it there.

When a new problem or issue presents itself, Andrew is very good at calling together the appropriate people, talking through the issue, and clarifying actions to be taken with milestones and

"I want a new way of looking at the problem. Particularly one that makes it seem minor and easy to solve."

timelines.   Then he begins to worry.   As he worries, he begins to talk with people in individual hallway conversations. After each conversation, he shoots out an email or calls some-one who is working on the problem and instructs them to do something new or different.   Some-times, his instruc-tions make great sense.   Other times, they send the individual off on a wild goose chase.   In many cases, his instructions have the sound of "If you would just do this, everything will be wonderful" attached to them.

As he tries to calm his old brain's worrying, Andrew lands on simple solutions.   He loses sight of what has already been done and simply looks for closure of any kind. His old brain drives him to shoot out "the answer" and then he feels finished. The feeling that a solution is at hand gives Andrew a brief respite from his worry.

As recipients of Andrew's emails, people find themselves pulled off of a good plan in order to chase information that often turns out to be a waste of time. Those who work for Andrew talk among themselves about how to avoid these conversations with him, because they seem to trigger his "if you'd just" approaches. Of course, they cannot predict when a conversation will do this, so they feel helpless in curtailing the process.

Simple solutions seduce us with a feeling of closure.

This creates a confusing situation for Andrew. He doesn't understand why his people aren't as excited about his "solutions" as he is. The reason, of course, is that most of the time he hasn't provided a solution, but rather just more unproductive work for his people. They see the wasted time. He is fooled by his old brain into seeing progress.

Pay Plans As Leadership Substitutes

As head of sales for a service organization, Tom feels, "It's all about the comp plan." He grew up in sales and has demonstrated (at least to himself) that "sales people are motivated by money." He believes it explains his own career path, and it informs his approach with his people. He plays a critical role for his organization every year in reviewing the goals and various elements of the sales compensation program and making recommendations.

Tom regularly complains about the compensation program for his sales people.   "It doesn't recognize how difficult this particular market is," or "This pay element is too low and doesn't get people to do what we want!" When his sales people misbehave and treat support staff poorly, he defends this toxic behavior. "We are here to make sales. The support staff can be replaced." The focus for Tom is clear and simple: the right money formula will drive the sales the business needs. Everything else blends into vague background noise.

"Sales figures don't lie. Stevens, hand over the big, foam, number one hand to Toelson."

Tom is trapped in the simple solution. He has narrowly defined success and all of its components into a single idea: that the compensation program motivates the behavior you want. He has simplified this part of the business to the point of ignoring the real complexity of having humans in the mix.

Avoiding the Seduction of Simplicity

A key characteristic of the old brain is that it is simplistic. Remember, a predator doesn't do much announcing before the pounce (the ones who did didn't get to make much of a contribution to their gene pool, either), so the old brain is attuned to small, simple inputs.

In addition, these adaptations arose before language evolved (even before the portion of our brain that creates language evolved), so the old brain operates without language.

Finally, we behave rapidly in response to threats. Rapid, in this case, is on the order of fractions of a second. Even much later on when logical structures evolved that drive our conscious thought, these more advanced structures operated secondarily to the old brain in threat situations.

As a result, the world appears to our old brains as clear cut and simple. All the while, keep in mind, without our having much, if any, awareness of the process.

In today's world, when our old brain is in charge, we feel that people are either "for" us or "against" us - something is a good thing or a bad thing. There is no room for compromise. There is no grey area. When we are voicing our opinions in these terms, we are likely riding an old brain wave.

One way to observe this in action in the workplace is to look for the presence of "either-or" thinking. With the old brain driving, people will often offer simplification of complex situations. "We either have to invest in new software or give up this market segment." It would be wonderful if business issues were so clear-cut as that.

The power of "AND" resides in your new brain.

Here we have an example of a situation where the business would be better served by new brain thinking about a complicated situation. The old brain is the power behind the "Tyranny of OR," which refers to our getting stuck with a choice between two polar alternatives, with no middle ground. The Tyranny of OR really means that we have stopped the critical new brain thinking that can move us forward. Instead we have given in to our old brain's simplification.

It is not that you never have to make a choice in business. You do, of course. Rather, the old brain moves to that choice too quickly, shutting down important critical thinking that can move your business ahead. It is this critical thinking that provides the subtlety and complexity usually required in business.

Another common example of old brain thinking is the excessively simplistic solution. "What we need is a good marketing plan," or "it's all about execution" are a couple that come to mind easily. The truth is, business is not easy and it is rarely simple, especially once one gets to the corporate level. The fact is, a successful business needs execution, marketing, good people, great strategy, and on and on. Good leadership usually requires complex thinking that is not served well by the old brain.

From an evolutionary perspective, this simplicity has served us well. In the midst of a dangerous situation, we don't get bogged down with analysis and vocabulary. We just take action. Once our "fear engine" gets revved up, all the systems necessary for us to defend ourselves, at least in a primitive environment, are primed for action. In the current context that means we get focused on simple solutions.

All progress is precarious, and the solution of one problem brings us face to face with another problem.
--Martin Luther King, Jr.

Another manifestation of the simplicity of the old brain is in its lack of detail awareness and comfort with generality. When the old brain is active, you often hear words like "always" and "never." There was no time or need for analyzing the possibilities of what could be causing the "rustle in the bushes."

Go with the "bush rustling always equals danger" equation and survive.

Most of us would agree that there is very little in life that is an "always" or "never" proposition, but that is a level of complexity that the old brain just does not handle effectively.

While we can adapt and respond with our old brains, it doesn't help us very much with thinking, planning, or clear communication.   It is therefore extremely difficult for our old brain to distinguish between what goes on in the real world outside of us and what goes on in our heads.   The critical thinking necessary to do good "reality testing" isn't available to our old brain.

We've all had the experience where we've had a heated argument with someone and we walk away muttering under our breath, even though the other person cannot hear us any longer. We continue the conversation in our heads, and often it can begin to feel much more satisfying than the real conversation. This is an example of our old brain driving behavior, as if it is actually doing something (continuing the conversation), but in fact is simply engaging in an internal dialogue where we can even fill in both sides and reach a conclusion that allows us to feel safe.

Most of us have also experienced a situation where we carry on a dialogue in our heads before our interaction with the other person has even begun, and we end up in quite a tizzy even though nothing has actually happened yet.   In this case, our old brain has created an emotional response to something that *has not occurred*.   The emotions feel very real to us, and we really become agitated.   For the old brain, the boundary between fantasy and reality is not at all clear.   Left exclusively to its own devices, the old brain easily becomes preoccupied with an interior focus.

What leader has not experienced a subordinate wound up like a cyclone because of an old brain internal dialogue that is buzzing around in his head rather than something that has actually transpired? As we interact with people like this, it seems clear that he really believes what he is experiencing. His old brain has convinced him that something dangerous is in the offing. And, as we all know, it is not that easy to talk him out of this.

When it feels like things are not going as we wish, easy answers feel good to us. We are drawn to the quick fix or immediate solution, the first answer coming to us that feels like a resolution. The pitfall here is that we can find ourselves pouncing on an "FBA" or "First Best Answer." When we are in old brain mode, we are looking for relief, a way of knowing we are safe. Once we hear a solution that begins to provide that relief, we rope it in and call it done!

Just because it comes naturally and easily doesn't mean it is a good idea.

Andrew is an example of this in action. He thrives on the FBA approach to calm his fears. He doesn't see that others are impacted in ways that prevent action. Tom has taken this a step further. He has adopted an FBA into a way of running his business unit.

What Can You Do?

The simplicity of the old brain is one of the hardest characteristics to pick up in ourselves. It feels as if we are doing good things, the *right* things, not the simple or even stupid thing! We can be helpful to others here, because we can spot the symptoms of old brain simplicity in them, but go on about our simple ways without awareness.

The wrong thing can feel so right!

Having someone point out that our solution is simple isn't very satisfying, of course. Consider some of the following action steps to overcoming the seduction of the old brain's simplicity.

- **Pay Attention to Your Own Language**

    Pay attention to whether you are using phrases like, "If only we could...." or "All we need is...." or "If we would just...." Also listen to yourself for words like "always" and "never." All of these are dead giveaways that the old brain is driving you toward a simplistic solution.

- **Clearly Define the Problem at Hand**

    Get the right people involved in defining what the problem is and solving it. Get many ideas about what to do. Not everyone will be in their old brains during these discussions. You could, of course, draw out other people's old brains with your own strong energy. But perhaps they will help calm your fears through critical thinking that you have not yet done. Andrew actually does this well, as a starting point.

- **Avoid "Figuring It Out"**

    Are you making a suggestion for action and feeling relief like you've "figured it out?" Here is where Andrew falls prey to his own fears in search of the comfort of a simple but final solution.

    Investigate with others what you may all be missing. When our old brain energy moves us to simple perspectives, we stop asking the critical questions that will help us move to better results. When you challenge yourself and others to do critical thinking, it is your new brain that responds. If you find, for any reason, that you are shortcutting this, that's a clue to which part of your brain is doing the driving.

• Write Out or Speak A Full Explanation of Your Solution

Put your full explanation in writing or say it clearly out loud. In order to do this, you must shift out of your old brain to find the language to express yourself. Avoid keeping your thinking all in your head, because the actual words we use and energy we express when we get out of our heads can help us move into our new brain. By writing out your explanation or speaking it fully, you may spot the simplicity of your solution.

• Question, Question, Question

Ask yourself questions like, "If this (FBA) solution does fix the problem, what will I expect to see done differently? Why?" Tie the new behavior to the solution in a way that makes clear sense. Avoid the "miracle" space - that place in your thought processes that is making big assumptions where you are unable to see how you and others can behave to make it happen.

Let's say we conduct the first line supervisor training. We expect morale to improve and negativity to diminish. How will we know that something from the training had an impact on this? This alone might cause us to begin to question our First Best Answer. Standard questions for critical thinking include:

- What will I expect to see after the training that I do not see now?
- How will I know something different is happening?

- When will I know that we have gotten the value of the training we expected?
- What are the benchmarks for success?

"I THINK YOU SHOULD BE MORE EXPLICIT HERE IN STEP TWO."

• Invite Others to Challenge You

Specifically ask others to find the flaws in your ideas. Even if it is a great idea, you can still ask, "What might keep this from working the way we think it will?" A big key here is this: Don't do it all yourself! Remember how selfish and self-centered the old brain is? Having others involved can take advantage of their ability to see our oversimplifications.

• Think Up Another Solution

Another great question to ask is "What else could we do that might affect this situation?" Challenge yourself and others to produce multiple solutions and choose among them after thorough consideration of each option. Challenge yourself and your team to come up with at least five (for example) options before you decide on a course of action.

If you are feeling that you do not have enough time to stop the old brain's simplification, then your old brain is influencing your actions.   You may have heard the comment from others that "we do not have time to do it right, but we have time to do it over."   Here is the brain source of that frustration.   Take the time!

11.
Leading From the Rearview Mirror

~~~~

Recall the last trip you took in your car. Where was your attention focused? If you are like most drivers, the vast majority of your attention is focused on the road ahead. There is the occasional glance at the speedometer and the other gauges on the dashboard. And there are the regular glances in the rearview mirror. This is standard good driving behavior. Why? Because most of what you have to deal with is in front of you. Turns, stoplights, cars entering the road from cross streets, bumps, hills, etc., are all in front of you.

The analogy is apt for the way we run our businesses. Most of what matters to our business is in front of us, not behind. We are often making decisions quickly in order to stay ahead of what our customers want and need from us. The needs of our people change and evolve. Our competitors aren't standing still either. So we are driving at a pretty fast clip. It makes no more sense to drive this "business" trip from the rearview mirror than it does to drive any trip in our car. Keeping our eyes on the road ahead is our best bet.

So why do we spend so much time looking in the rearview mirror? Our natural tendency to look at problems draws our attention to the past, and it may feel like we are doing something valuable. But really, most of us believe Einstein was right, the past is over. There are no "do-overs." Every opportunity for change and improvement is in the future.

Stuck in a Serious Rut

Christopher, the CEO of a global consulting firm, has a clear picture in his head about what is true in the marketplace, how to best run the business, and what people should be doing in order to be successful. In this he is like most chief executives. Unfortunately for Christopher, this clear picture is based on what the business was like 20 years ago.

Since then, the services provided by his firm have been significantly displaced by technology solutions. The competitive landscape has changed as well. There are many more very capable competitors playing in Christopher's space now.

Christopher is stuck in a business model that, although once very successful, is pulling the firm into a death spiral. As he watches the performance of the business deteriorate, his old brain gets increasingly active. This activity exacerbates his tendency to look to the past for solutions, managing through his rearview mirror.

To make matters worse, these tired solutions are simplistic and no longer helpful to the front line of the business. Here are some of Christopher's favorite bromides:

- "If every consultant would just bill one more hour per week to one client, we would be profitable enough to pay bonuses to everyone." Christopher has been telling his people this for over 15 years.

- "We have products and services that the market wants. All you have to do is get in front of clients and they will buy." When Christopher company was leading the market in products and services, this had some truth to it.

For people working for him, this persistent view of the world from the past leaves only two approaches to take in dealing with Christopher: You can tell him what he wants to hear so he will get off your case. This means that he does not have to face any realities outside of his current mindset, so nothing ever changes. Or you can take a chance of having your career derailed and being belittled ruthlessly in front of others by telling him what you believe will be helpful to hear to run the business better.

©Marty Bucella www.martybucella.com

Time Travel Inc.

"How about last Thursday? Is last Thursday good for you?"

Obviously, Christopher has some serious old brain activity that drives his leadership. In fact, he has gotten himself locked into these stories because there was some kernel of truth at one point, when the company was small and the services offered were leading edge. He likes those kernel of truths more than facing the reality of today. His company has gone from a growing, thriving leading-edge organization to an old fashioned, stodgy, slow moving and failing one.

The "Watch Out" Call

Jackson recently took over the operations function of a large distilling operation. He had a similar background and experience with another firm, and had some clear ideas about how to best operate for optimal output. He spent several weeks learning the history and current situation of the plant, and then began to have regular meetings to change the way things were going.

Jackson was very good at pointing out two things to his people: how he had seen similar work done in the past that was successful, and what his people had done in the past that was not successful. "How else are we going to improve, if we don't watch out for past mistakes and take advantage of successes?" he would ask.   Jackson's clear mindset was looking at the business from the rearview mirror.

Soon, operating results began to suffer.   Accidents increased, although fortunately no one was seriously injured.   Rumors of "poor morale" began to surface, although when Jackson investigated them, people's acknowledgement of it typically did not include any helpful information.

In order to turn the situation around, Jackson doubled his efforts at pointing out what was going wrong and "calling people on the carpet" to change. Over time, he began to frequently emphasize that certain people "always" or "never" took certain action (you may recognize the old brain's simplicity at work here). He used these terms to both punish and reward the behavior he saw.

As "old" solutions failed to deliver results, Jackson's old brain continued to fuel his intensity to a nearly fanatical level. Ultimately, people who worked for Jackson began to feel that no matter what they did, they could not please him.   As they withheld the discretionary effort necessary for real success, performance overall continued to decline in a self-reinforcing plummet into failure.

Keeping Our Eyes on the Road

Both Christopher and Jackson got caught up in their old brain's tendency to look to the past. Recall that in Gur's time, going back to where you had found berries previously or avoiding the watering hole at certain times because of past predator run-ins was critical to survival. So remembering and effectively acting on past experiences keeps us feeling safe.

Our ability to imagine a future (so we can look out the windshield) was in its infancy in Gur's time. Because survival was the focus of life actions, the only future Gur and his clan members could imagine was a catastrophic one, driven by very real fears of death and dismemberment. In the case of this primitive gatherer, if he had been threatened by a predator, once he removed himself from danger and his old brain had calmed down, he resumed his search for food. He did not think about the fruit that might grow next season. He was only looking for food and safety for today.

The survival value of learning from the past far outweighed the value of imagining what next year, or even next week, might look like. There was no long term activity going on - no farming or other organized efforts - to draw attention to a changing future. Gur and the clan took advantage of what was available to them at any given time, and avoided danger.

A view of the future began to form as we evolved from the hunter/gatherer to an agricultural society. Long term weather patterns, crop rotation, soil depletion and other elements were influenced by our behavior, and we developed a capacity to think in a forward fashion to improve our fates. Looking to the past became a way of learning how to have the biggest impact, and experimentation resulted in both wins and losses that reinforced our thinking and brain evolution. When we are able to see how well things are going, we feel safe. But a problem arises, we become fearful, and the past sings its song of safety.

In addition, the old brain has no way to distinguish the recent past from the distant past. It is all compressed into one emotional constellation. Christopher's hold on his 20-year rearview story is an example of this. Christopher is smart and capable, and yet he was not able to maintain a clear understanding of what had changed over time when his old brain focused him on the past. This idea worked back then, so why not now? No answer could be heard without revealing a potential catastrophe.

When we get in an argument and become emotional, we are likely to bring examples and issues from the distant past that are similar and use them in the current moment, even though they do not legitimately belong there. These past, painful events spring readily to mind when we are agitated, even though we might not have thought of them without the emotional stimulus. The pain of past events is added to the pain of current events, so when we are emotionally agitated, we may dredge up old events and use them (not necessarily intentionally) to stoke the fires of our emotional response to the current situation.

Here is a useful rule of thumb: any particular incident of emotional arousal is only *10%* contemporary and approximately *90%* historical. Imagine an iceberg, with the bulk of the demonstrated emotion caused by situations hidden by time!

This is one of the reasons it is so hard to engage in a rational discussion when our old brain is humming. Again,

Christopher's dangerous behavior when his story was challenged emerged from emotional energy stoked and maintained over a very long time.

The value to us in this case is the energizing force brought to bear in the current moment to resolve a problem. It creates an elevated systemic response to the moment. In simpler times, that extra energy might be what was needed for that individual to prevail.

In any particular incident of emotional arousal, only 10% of the emotion is contemporary. The other 90% is historical.

This can sometimes be true in contemporary business, but optimal business success rarely comes from giving in to the strongest emotional response. In fact, the more dramatically emotional someone is in a contemporary setting, the less likely a long term, effective and thoughtful approach will be considered.

Recalling our driving analogy, you do want to glance in the rearview mirror regularly, to be sure you know what you need to know to move forward safely, right? When we are driving, the view out the rearview mirror changes – suddenly there are new vehicles on the road, others are passing us or we are passing them, so the "past" changes. We can take action (speed up, slow down, change lanes) that influences the future. In our real business life, the past is done, the view does not change, and we truly cannot return to the past for a do-over.

Looking to the past can be valuable if there is something to learn. It does require some careful attention to a future perspective, however, or we easily fall into the same trap as Christopher and Jackson.

Optimal business success rarely comes
from giving into the strongest
emotional response.

Once we have squeezed out every drop of learning available from the past, our view of it is likely to change. What looked like a mistake may still look like a mistake, but the people involved often look simply fallible rather than inept or cruel. Our stories change from someone being stupid, uncaring or malicious to attributes that are less scary, more predictable, and ultimately more helpful to us on our path to success.

What Can You Do?

How can we avoid the past? Let us acknowledge clearly that you *cannot avoid the past*. The odds of accomplishing this, even with a good deal of personal insight and intensive therapy, are not high! However, being a great leader takes effort each and every day, in each situation, mindful of our own contribution, in order to minimize these natural constraints to be the best leader we can be.

Being a great leader takes effort,
each and every day.

Here are some things you can do to allow the past to inform the future, and move forward effectively.

- Practice Emotional Self-Control

  On any given day, problems arise that require our attention. Some will generate strong emotions that push us into old brain responses. Practice catching your emotional reaction before it is visible.

Emotions work in a particular way, as shown in the graphic below. You have an unconscious emotional reaction to some event. You then "feel" it in one or more parts of your body - your stomach feels queasy or gets "butterflies," your head feels full and pulsing, your hands ache, your throat closes up. Then, you do (lean forward) or say ("What!!??!!") something that demonstrates you have had an emotional reaction. Sometimes, we are not even aware of it until someone points it out ("You don't have to yell at me!").

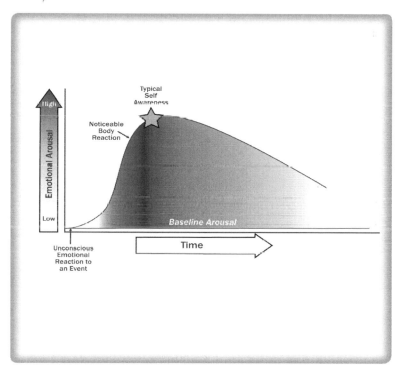

The better you get at "catching" the feeling somewhere in your body so that your conscious awareness is earlier in the emotional "build," the easier it is to rein in your visible response.   This gives you time to calm down and decide, using your new brain, to do the right thing.

Look for cues from others to help yourself become more aware of early indicators. You can even ask others to help you with this. Often people are reluctant to make comments without invitation. For sure, there is information out there that you can take advantage of.

Once you have been given some cue information, pay attention.   Do not worry if you miss a cue for several minutes.   This is a learning process that takes practice. Once you find yourself exclaiming "Shoot!" to yourself when you realize that a cue came and went 30 seconds ago, you are on your way to real positive change.   Stay with it. The ability to manage your emotional reactions internally is a key element to great leadership.

• Perform an Autopsy Without Blame

Think of the past as "dead" for a moment.   When do you perform an autopsy on the dead? When you do not understand the cause of death, of course.

If the death resulted from "natural causes," there is no need to review the circumstances.   Things did not go as you'd like.   What do you want to have happen now, to get the work back on track? A review of the past will be a waste of time and energy, and will have a longer term negative impact on those involved, because it is likely to feel punishing.

"Natural causes" means that either it is obvious what went wrong or it doesn't matter what went wrong. But if you are surprised or confused by a situation and it is not a freak of nature, determining the cause of death is a focus on learning that is the most likely to prevent similar future situations.

An *Autopsy Without Blame*, which is the hallmark of the intentional leadership conversation, is intended to investigate all the important elements of a situation to reach a coherent, truthful picture.   There are typically four categories of information to pursue:

What Did We Want to Have Happen?

As previously discussed, it is most helpful to begin with what is most important.   What really matters, and what did we want to have happen so that we were getting after what matters?   Start with known intentions (we wanted everyone to be safe, we wanted the plant to continue running, we wanted to follow all appropriate procedures, we wanted this one unit taken off-line for repairs).

Include any unknown or unstated intentions that surface now because of what you now know (we wanted Pete and Jennifer to take the lead on it, we wanted Sammy to learn how to do it for next time, we wanted to reinforce a new approach to working together).

Capture as many intentions as possible, even if some of them do not seem important at the time.

What Worked Well?

Since you expected it to go well, investigate what worked the way you thought it would and the way you wanted it to work.   Include what worked even better than you thought it would or wanted it to!

There are a few reasons for taking this action as the step after clarifying what you wanted to have happen.

* It highlights for everyone involved that some things did go well (in fact, often a lot of things did go well). This will sometimes begin to draw people's attention

away from any overwhelming feelings of blame and shame.

* It also works to put people in a positive frame of mind for viewing what did not go as planned.
* By recognizing the reality of what worked well, a clear picture begins to form about where a problem may have arisen. There may even be some things that were pleasant surprises.

An additional value of this part of the autopsy without blame is that you talk clearly about what is viewed as success, and people get a better picture in their heads about what success looks like.   This increases the likelihood that they will replicate it going forward.

What Will We Do Differently Next Time?
Although this may seem like the equivalent of "what didn't work well," this is intended as a *future* question. Taking a future perspective is more likely to keep everyone involved processing from their new brains, so you will get better analysis and more creative thinking about how to do well in the future (the only place you can exert some control).   More importantly, it may not be possible to replicate this set of events in the future, given that time has passed and things have changed, so it maintains a "reality" perspective.

Finally, the question approached in this way minimizes blame and shame by allowing people to talk about doing their best *next time*. If people want to take responsibility for any unfortunate actions on their part during this conversation, others can graciously accept it as acknowledgement of learning for the future. Here is the watch-out, however. Move the conversation back to the future as quickly as possible, so that the old brain does not engage.

What Did We Learn?
Summarize what the entire conversation has been about. What did we learn about how to have the right intentions, how to do the right things, how to be our best? Where are we more capable now than we were before? End with a clear articulation of what the future will likely bring, given this learning. Again, a clear picture of what success looks like leads to that success.

- ## Choose Your Battles

If issues arise because of "natural causes," it is time to move on. If moving on causes you stress, try forgiveness. A definition of forgiveness that can be very helpful is this:

Forgiveness is letting go of all hope for a better past.
-Unknown

Fighting a battle to change the past is futile. Fighting a battle that cannot be won is unwise. If reviewing an issue will simply reinforce to people how things cannot change, you have reinforced the wrong message. Choose your battles to address how the future can improve.

- ## Tell People What You Want, Not What You Don't Like

As good as it may feel, it is simply not helpful to tell people what they are doing that you do not like. This is a slippery slope into "me" thinking.

Instead, clearly state your future intentions or desires. Say clearly to people what it is you want to see happen, not what you don't like about the past. Resist that very tempting flicker in your rearview mirror. It is just a tweak of your old brain.

Often it is helpful to take a brief time-out to allow ourselves to calm down enough to talk about what we want. After all, our old brain is most intent on spotting the problem and then blaming someone for it. Working through a brief script in your head before you speak can help you stay in the future, where real change happens.

If someone specifically asks for "feedback" and it feels to you like they want to know what you don't like, take a breath.   The individual may be open to hearing your information, and if so it may be helpful.   But danger lurks, so tread lightly.   Here are some things to think about:

- What clear message do you want to reinforce about what is important?

- What specific behavior (action or words) did this person contribute that seemed in conflict with what is important?

- How can you turn this situation into a learning opportunity for both you and this person, so that you have increased the likelihood that they will do something more effectively in the future and you will know how to be helpful to them in the future?

If you stumble through this set of questions, either you are still stewing on the situation in your old brain, or the conversation will not be helpful. However, if you want to have an Intentional Leadership Conversation, now might be the time.

12.
My Story Is True, And Yours Isn't!

We have all been faced with the colleague who just can't seem to give in. You know, the person who just bulldogs a position until others either wilt and give in or simply leave the meeting. Perhaps you have even been accused of being this person at one time or another.

In business, we are expected to demonstrate strong advocacy for our positions. In fact, people who can't make a strong business case often don't make it too far up the food chain in most companies. But what about the person who just takes it too far, when advocacy becomes obstinacy?

Part of the challenge of business is getting people together, engaging their new brains, and enabling the critical thinking that drives business success. When one or more of the players gets too invested in one particular solution, the going gets tough. Critical thinking ends up on the sidelines as the participants in the meeting up the intensity of their attacks and the "stubborn" player hunkers down in defense of his position.

Obstinacy is poor advocacy.

While this is a common business model, it is certainly not optimal, and usually not effective at all. We end up with winners, losers, grudges, and, in general terms, very agitated old brains.

At the heart of these challenges are two critical drivers.

- We have a critical need to create a coherent story, or narrative, for our life and the lives of those around us. This is a never-ending process that operates whether we want it to or not. Undoubtedly, this ability to create a compelling story is critical to our thinking processes. But sometimes it is simply not helpful.

- We have an abiding sense of "rightness" about our stories. That is, we feel strongly that our particular sense of the world is indeed true and real. Other versions of reality seem stupid, uninformed, even hostile. They threaten us because they make us feel unsafe.

Great leadership demands that we first move outside our own stories and that we challenge our belief in our own "rightness." Once we have successfully done this, we can help others do the same.

May The Best Story Win!

Let's meet Jeff. Jeff is the CEO of a technology company with very innovative hardware and software solutions for highly demanding installations. The key challenge facing the company is revenue. The top line is lagging behind the designs and developments in engineering. The sales team isn't getting in front of enough customers and isn't booking the sales to keep pace with the growth demands of the business.

The regular sales meetings include Jeff, the sales leader, five regional sales professionals, a representative from engineering, and the marketing leader. These participants are highly motivated to be successful and consider themselves to be professionals in their respective areas. As you can imagine, a major focus for each meeting is, "What's going on with the top line? Why aren't we booking more sales?"

Each participant has a strong point of view concerning the shortfall. Jeff pushes hard on one key metric, face-to-face customer meetings. Based on his long experience in the business, and his considerable success in making key sales in the past as the business was growing, he is passionately committed to driving sales through attention to this metric. He presents a comprehensive explanation as to why his story is the right one at this point in time.

Of course, the regional sales people have a different story. All five strongly believe that a lack of more professional marketing support materials is the critical constraint. Each salesperson presents compelling stories of actual prospect situations where these materials would have made the difference. The energy shown by the salespeople in advocating their case is impressive.

Marketing, as you can easily imagine, has yet another story. That version of the truth is that the sales people aren't familiar with the information on the website. And, they are also not sufficiently conversant with the intricacies of the technology solutions to be persuasive advocates in front of potential customers.

As the meeting unfolds, each story is told, and sometimes told again. After a while, though, a subtle change begins to take place. The focus moves from seeking a solution that will benefit the business as a whole to finding flaws with the stories of others, and to bolstering one's own story. In the end, the energy of the meeting is ultimately squandered in a battle over whose story is right rather than an effective pursuit of business solutions. It is no surprise that the top line continues to languish.

Building A Culture Of Giving Up

As a regional head for a national construction firm, Kirk is responsible for delivering profit, timely completion, and customer satisfaction on all construction projects undertaken by the firm in his region of the United States. This is a challenging position with a wide range of very large building projects under way in several states.

Kirk's region is struggling to meet goals on all three key metrics: profitability, timely completion, and customer satisfaction.

It is Kirk's strong belief that there are critical differences in the labor pool in his region that make the company's standard approach to labor management inappropriate. Rather than use multiple sub-contractors as the company business model demands, Kirk believes hiring workers directly onto the company payroll is a requirement for success. He continually engages in battles with his boss and national HR to get permission to change this part of the business model for his region. He regularly sends his impassioned pleas up the corporate chain, to no avail.

So strongly does Kirk believe in his story that most of the meetings with his direct reports are just a reprise of his latest attempt to influence upward. He inundates his people with stories of his corporate battles, always lost. With Kirk so caught up in the truth and rightness of his story, there is no room left for his own team to come up with alternatives that might actually benefit the business he is trying to run. Any energy one of his managers might have to make effective changes is always overwhelmed by Kirk's intense investment in his own rightness. After a while, his team just gives up and goes back to the daily grind of surviving in an environment where goals are never met.

The Myth of Venting

Dave is the CEO of a niche financial services firm. With a history of solid profitability, the key challenges for Dave's firm is growing the top line more aggressively and gaining market share in the face of tough competition.

Lately Dave has been feeling as if he doesn't have enough time to think through the critical decisions in marketing and product development that his business requires. In a review of Dave's calendar, he has many, many individual meetings with not only his direct reports, but also with folks a level or two below them.

Dave's explanation is that he values an open door policy as a leader. He welcomes the opportunity to meet with the people in his organization and demonstrate his personal commitment to their success. These are admirable intentions, to be sure. But what was really happening in these meetings? "Venting" explains Dave. "People come in with a problem or issue and I allow them to vent."

Dave truly believes that this venting process helps people get through the issue, relieves the emotional tension, and builds a stronger bond with him as leader of the company.

> ## Triangulation is a sub-optimal approach to communication.

What Dave is really doing, however, is reinforcing the stories people bring to him. By letting people vent, he is helping them stay stuck in their story. Almost any action he takes short of arguing with them reinforces a story that isn't working for them right then. People complain about other people, complain about company policies, and even complain about things that aren't going well at home.

With no attempt to challenge these stories, Dave misses an opportunity to change the focus from the past to the future. He misses opportunities to de-personalize issues. And, perhaps most critically, Dave becomes the third leg of a triangle. By venting to Dave, people avoid having the crucial conversations with others involved that would more effectively resolve the issue.

The result of Dave's policy toward venting is a lot of negative energy in the hallways, fueled by personal resentment, disappointment, and no real movement on critical issues. People are trapped in the past, with a resulting deflection of energy that would be better spent pursuing the business agenda.

Our Storytelling Machine

We know that there was a huge evolutionary advantage to figuring out what others were thinking. That is, humans became good at creating stories about people and the world around them.

When our old brain is in charge, we increase our storytelling intensity. Storytelling occurs all the time. However, our storytelling intensifies when we become fearful. Our old brains quickly and effectively weave simple explanations for external events that allow us to feel safe. These stories take on a feeling of reality and rightness, a "true explanation," quickly. As we calm down, we take the basic story and add to it, with both our old and new brains, and eventually our story becomes truth to us.

Consider a "risk matrix." Imagine again that you are a person in the bush at the dawn of humanity and you hear a noise. There are four possible outcomes for you, each with different value to you.

- If the noise really is a danger, you can flee immediately and be safe. This is a "correct" response.

- If the noise is not really a danger, you can continue on your way with no flight response and be safe. This is also a "correct" response.

- If the noise is not a danger, you can flee anyway. This is an "incorrect" response which is usually called a False Positive. The cost of this "error" is minimal in this case, perhaps mild embarrassment for bolting for no good reason.

		Response	
		Correct	Incorrect
Danger?	Yes	Flee, be safe	No reaction, high cost of error (False Negative)
	No	No reaction, be safe	Flee, low cost of error (False Positive)

- If the noise does represent a danger and yet you fail to flee. This is also an "incorrect" response which is usually called a False Negative. The cost of this error is quite high, possibly fatal.

It is no stretch of the imagination to see that we are strongly evolved to believe our assessments of danger are true. Often, we do not let go of this belief without a real fight.

While the stories we create feel right and true to us, we can undermine our own good intentions by falling prey to these fantasies and tricking ourselves into thinking we have the real truth when we only have our story. Our old brain will provide us with very strong emotional cues that reinforce to us that we "know" what is right and true. But, this sense of rightness is just our old brain in action. It is not connected to reality in any proportion to the strength of the feeling.

We are strongly evolved to believe our assessments of danger are true.

Sometimes, when we are faced with a problem or a task, we worry and fret about it. If we carry on with this for some time, we can actually begin to think that we really did something – perhaps even that we did, in fact, complete the task. As we worry and play out different scenarios in our fantasies, we are making comparisons with events that have occurred in the past that may or may not be similar. The rumination on these past events allows some of the sense of completion from them to "rub off" in a manner of speaking onto the current event we are facing. So, in the end, we feel like we have made progress when we have not.

In business today, this commonly shows up in not accomplishing goals. A person makes a commitment to accomplish a specific task by a specific date and then commences the worrying process. Next thing she knows, her boss is asking her for a status report, and she is cornered. However, she has some great stories to tell about why no or little progress has been made. This is the value that springs from her previous ruminations, when she got stuck feeling as if she'd already finished something that she had not even started.

In the stories told previously in this chapter, we have three motivated leaders who have been successful enough in the past to move into positions of serious responsibility. Yet, key business challenges remain unmet. Rather than letting our own old brains lead us to a conclusion of ineptitude on their parts, let's try a new brain approach and critically examine what is going on here.

All humans have a powerful, pervasive, and persistent drive to create a story about themselves and the world around them, a coherent life narrative. This is not a process we get to choose. Our stories are created and in place often before we are even aware of them.

We are relentless storytelling machines!

If you ask Jeff, Kirk, or Dave what is going on, they will have a perfectly reasonable story to explain not only their own actions but the actions of those around them. They didn't get where they are without the ability to tell these stories in a compelling way.

With no real conscious intention, we create stories all day long. Stories about ourselves, our situation, and the people around us. These stories come with motives, goals, interconnections, and anticipated outcomes. So, for example, when Dave talks about his venting sessions, he has explanations for his behavior and all of these explanations are well reasoned. In addition, he has stories about how his people are thinking and feeling as a result. Not just casual comments, but well fleshed out narratives of what these meetings really mean to his people.

The critical point to understand here is that these stories are just that: stories. These stories are not reality. Most times our stories are highly coherent and plausible. If they were not, others would judge us to be crazy or at least very odd. Still, we can never know what is really going on in the heads of others. We can never really know all the facts. When we take our stories to represent reality, we risk ending up like Dave, Kirk, and Jeff, stuck in a suboptimal situation.

In addition, if our stories are not helpful, if they do not move us forward in a productive, efficient and helpful way, then they are no use to us. It does not matter how "true" our story is. Most would agree that the sun will, indeed, come up tomorrow. It's a good story, based on fact and expansive experience by all. If we are locked in a room with no windows, it may not be a helpful story.

It feels sooooooo good to be right!

In each case, Dave, Kirk and Jeff intended to move themselves and others forward in a productive, efficient and helpful way. Unfortunately, our intentions really don't matter that much here. These three leaders all have the best of intentions. Yet they are stuck in stories that are not working for them. And so are their people.

Why don't we just let go of our stories and open our minds to a range of alternatives? The answer lies in another troublesome quirk of our old brain. We really, really believe our stories are right!

The feeling of rightness all of us experience is extremely potent. It makes letting go of our stories so, so difficult. So difficult, in fact, that we usually don't. Jeff, Kirk, and Dave aren't letting go. They believe in their hearts they are right. They have that deep in the gut, fire in the belly, unassailable feeling that they are right and that their stories are true. At Jeff's sales meetings, the issue has become not what is best for business but whose story is right.

Unfortunately, everyone feels equally strongly about their own story. The stronger the advocacy of each individual, the stronger the defense on the part of others, and the stronger their attacks become, because, after all, they are right! Remember that the old brain is territorial. These challenges to the feeling of rightness are experienced, in the old brain, as territorial challenges that merit a fierce resistance.

Consider this: even if your story is right, if sticking to it is causing suboptimal results in your life, then your story is not helpful! The degree of feeling of rightness is unrelated to the external truth of the situation. It comes from your old brain, which as we know is weak in the logic and reality-testing realms.

The feeling of rightness often precedes the data to support our position.

As the clever thinking beings that we are, we convince ourselves that our story is a well reasoned, clearly thought out, rational analysis. This is, in itself, just another story. Often the reverse is true. That is, we have a feeling about what is right first. Then we seek out or make up information to support our feeling of rightness. Finally, in an elegant evolutionary gift, our old brain transmutes this into a reverse timeline so we feel the thinking came first and the feeling followed. The powerful feeling of rightness naturally follows.

What Can You Do?

All of our storytelling skill and propensity presents several critical learning points for a leader. Here are some actions you can take to resist the feeling of rightness in your stories to allow you, and others, to continue to learn and do things differently.

- ### Recognize It's a Story

   We will all be more effective if we understand the process. If you find yourself strongly supporting a position, your own or others, consciously remember that it's just a story. If you find yourself strongly disagreeing with someone else, remember consciously that you each have your own stories. Be intentional about recognizing that we are telling ourselves and others stories, and investing energy in how right we are.

• Let Go

Holding on to our stories is often not helpful. Step away and be objective about what is going on around you and within you. If you are

unhappy, frustrated, or fearful, your story is contributing to the situation. Learn when to let go of a story and create one that will work better for you.

In Jeff's case, he has some really good stories where the truth plays a role. So do his people. If Jeff could have let go of his story long enough to consider this, he may have come up with a story that said: "We aren't getting what we want. We don't really know why, although we all have some good ideas about it. Let's see if we can come up with a new story that does not have any one to blame."

• Respect the Right of Others to Have Their Stories

Others feel just as strongly as you do that they are right. They have just as much right to do so as you do! If someone else's story sounds wrong to you, you have several choices, some more respectful than others. Disrespectful choices include arguing with the content of the story, deriding the person as an idiot for coming up with it, or even laughing out loud.

Respectful choices include hearing them out without comment, asking questions to understand their thinking better, or simply moving the conversation to a more productive place by asking "What do you want to have happen in the long run?" This question often helps you see where you and the other person have similar intentions, if not stories.

• Create a New Story

Because your feeling of rightness is artificial, you can challenge it. Ask yourself what you want and what it might look like when you get it. Create a story around other people that gives them positive motives. See what story begins to get you different and better results, and stick with that story until it appears that it is no longer working.

Let's look at Kirk's situation again. Kirk's current story - that hiring workers directly onto the company payroll is a requirement for success - may be true, but it is not helpful to him or his team. He might benefit from talking with other leaders in the organization who are working with contractors successfully, to learn about different viewpoints.

Let's say he decides that there is a different approach and he wants to find it. This is the beginning of a new story. From here, he can use his best analytical thinking and invite others to help him. He can let go of his defensive, "I'm right, others are wrong" discussions with his staff, and help them, instead, learn how to deal effectively with the reality of the company. The company, his team and Kirk will benefit from a change of story.

Storytelling is one of the greatest tools we have.   It differentiates us from all other living things, it allows us to make sense of the world so that we can make progress in all areas of our lives, and it helps us feel safe.   Allow your storytelling to work for this good and not get in your way. Remember, it's just your story.

13.
Win One for the "Gipper"!

George Gipp, a star player on the Notre Dame football team in the 1930s, fell ill. Shortly before he died, Gipp asked his coach, Knute Rockne, to inspire the team when things were going badly for them, to "win one for the Gipper." A 1940s movie raised the phrase to a new level, and its star, Ronald Reagan, was given the nickname Gipper. He used the same quote during his election campaign for U.S. President.

So far, although we can admit that there are very important reasons for what happens in the processing of our old brains, the main message has been "watch out." Lest it seem that the old brain is nothing but a reservoir of bad motives and behaviors, there is another side to all this.

The old brain processes *all* our emotions. Remember that 90% of this processing is apparently aimed at dealing primarily with fear-based situations, where we feel threatened in some way.

This ties into our "negative" emotions - anger, frustration, disappointment, feelings of betrayal, and the like.

But the old brain also processes our positive emotions, which are just as important and compelling. It was important, at times, to get excited and enthusiastic about some things in our primitive environment. After all, those positive emotions serve to energize us for what were then important tasks. Our passion, enthusiasm, and excitement also stem from our old brains. What happens when we bring these positive emotions to the table in our work? If you have seen it in action, you know it can be good!

Our positive emotions can be just as energizing as our negative ones.

The Passionate Leader

Here is a story that will be familiar to anyone in a service businesses. William was brought in to grow the business of a small regional consulting firm. Because of his past experiences and his view of the world, he knew what he wanted. He immediately implemented his "three questions." Regardless of what issue came before him or what problems he encountered, he asked these questions until he got an answer that mattered. If he got no answer that mattered, then the issue did not matter and he moved on. His questions were:

> "How does this best serve our clients?"

> "How does this make us better so we can serve our clients better in the future?"

> "How does this help us run the business most efficiently, so we can best serve our clients?"

By asking these questions relentlessly, William helped people remember at all times what the business was all about. The point of these questions was to focus his people on the heart of the business, which was client service. By sharing his passion for this pursuit, William was eliciting some excitement and passion from his people. This elicited passion served to energize his team and align them in a common cause, a cause that others were proud to be part of.

William began every formal meeting asking for stories about client service that either reinforced how it was done well or helped people understand how hard it could be. He engaged people in conversations that brought the important issues to light, so that people felt they could be their best with their clients. These conversations also helped people understand how to avoid losing sight of what was important in their daily work.

In the past, this business consisted of the pursuit of new client projects, for which a consultant got credit and therefore compensation, and billable hours, also a key component in compensation for consultants. This resulted in consultants focusing on how hard they were working and how much business they were bringing in. This worked in the short term - the hard work brought in business, and hard work put dollars in the company's coffers faster.

However, this approach also built territorial thinking, because people did not want to give up what they could get even if it was to the client's benefit. This approach also built up resentment when people worked long hours and still had to hear clients complain. There were other downsides to this approach, and it was hard for people to feel that they were doing something that really mattered.

The benefits of a passionate pursuit of a worthy mission, client service, were not only more projects and billable hours, but also clients who noticed the difference in the way they were treated.

The traditional benefits followed the passionate pursuit rather than the other way around. Delighted clients, delighted because of the passion and energy of those serving them, created more business for the firm. This belies the fallacy of the traditional model that focuses service providers on dollars and hours.

Profit and growth are the applause that comes after you have done the right things.

Passionless Pursuit of Profit

Joseph is the CEO of a large energy firm. He understands the business and has a keen mind for determining how best to serve the stakeholders of the organization. He presents facts and figures in ways that most people, regardless of their level of knowledge about the business, can understand.

The problem is that there is no compelling vision or passion in evidence. Joseph's story about what he does is simple: it's his job to keep the company profitable, so that the stock price stays high and dividends are paid to shareholders. This is his fiduciary responsibility, and he takes it very seriously - as he should.

Joseph also believes strongly in taking care of his employees, and he demonstrates that in his decisions. He attends all company activities that are appropriate for him to attend, and he is personable and likable to employees. He "walks the halls" and asks how people are doing, and he reinforces the importance of volunteer work in the many communities where his company does business.

But when asked what they think Joseph finds important, employees will almost uniformly answer "Keep costs low so profits are high and shareholders are happy."

The company has gone, under Joseph's leadership, from a thriving organization to one limping along and fighting for survival. Obviously, times are bad and Joseph's leadership isn't the only element at play. But what is true is that Joseph demonstrates limited passion and he engages employees on a very limited basis.

Limited passion means limited engagement.

Joseph is good at determining what to do and communicating that clearly in ways that stimulate appropriate action. What he is missing is any explanation of what matters and why. He has provided employees little that they can genuinely care about, and therefore make a passionate commitment to.

Driving Business Success With Passion and Enthusiasm

As the seat of all emotion, the old brain is, of course, responsible for our positive emotions. When we get enthusiastic and energized, that is our old brain in action. When we attempt to arouse passionate commitment in others (and ourselves), we are attempting to elicit positive old brain activity. That burning desire to achieve or please a customer is based in our old brain. So, there are certainly times when we want that to happen.

With that said, though, keep in mind that when you are enthusiastically energized, your old brain is still the driver and the risks that we have outlined throughout this book still apply. That is, for example, you are no better at critical thinking when zealously engaged than when you are angry. People around you probably like it better, but the business results are often only marginally better.

This is worth restating in this way: we are just as simple, selfish, territorial, blaming and past-focused when we are enthusiastic and passionate, as we are when we are angry or frustrated!

We are just as simple, selfish, territorial, blaming and past focused when we are enthusiastic and passionate as we are when we are angry or frustrated.

As we've pointed out previously, about 90% of the wiring in the old brain is allocated to dealing with fear. Even though we are now at the top of the food chain and seldom deal with truly dangerous environments, our old brains still predispose us toward the negative. Our regular and frequently consciousness of this one fact can go far to help us being our best.

In contemporary leadership situations, we walk a fine line. On one side we wish to generate some positive old brain activity, such as enthusiasm. On the other side are a host of responses that have negative consequences. It is a slippery slope that leads one from generating passionate team commitment to creating a hostile "us against them" swirl. It is great to be proud of your team, your department, your company, or your country. When that leads to demonizing non-members, the negative aspects of the old brain have gained the upper hand and the result is almost always less grand than we had hoped.

From the deepest desires often comes the deadliest hate.
--Socrates

Here's what is important about all this information about the old brain: there are predictable behaviors that come from old brain processing. We can recognize them. We can take action as leaders that will help people complete their old brain processing or turn it toward a better outcome. Or better yet, we can learn to lead in such a way as to minimize and optimize old brain activity.

What Can You Do?

Although it is flirting with the old brain's less than effective drivers, drawing on your own passion and determining what really matters is a key to great leadership. The difference it makes when people are inspired to be great is phenomenal. Here are some actions you can take to tap this powerful and positive part of the old brain to engage the best from others.

"We don't know why we make these, so we're hoping to find people who don't know why they buy them."

• Figure Out For Yourself What Matters

There is plenty of information out there on developing a compelling vision. The core of it is this: what really matters? If you run a company that offers products to its customers, it's possible that what really matters is that your customers really, really like your product. Or perhaps what really matters is that customers want your products because they are inexpensive and easy to obtain.

There are any number of ways to determine what really matters, but until *you* see it clearly, it will be hard for others to do so.   Ask yourself why you get up in the morning, every morning, and head off to do this work. Your own passion is a good place to look for cues to what might engage others.

- ## Decide What the Key Levers Can Be

If our customers buy our products because they are inexpensive and easy to obtain, the key levers to achieving excellence are predictable.   How do we keep costs down? How do we balance our desire to limit our costs with the obvious impact on distribution costs, defects, and quality?

Are there ways to think about cost and distribution that create opportunities for our customers, such as new distribution channels, new inputs to the process, or different processing approaches that allow us to maintain or improve the position in the marketplace for our products? Using the power of our analytic new brain *follows* the clear definition of what matters.

- ## Talk About What Matters and Ask Others to Do the Same

Beware the barrenness of a busy life.
--Socrates

Make your grand mission a part of every business conversation. When people get caught up in daily problem solving, ask them to make connections to what matters. Perhaps your technology upgrade needs are causing people to balk because of cost.   Ask them to think about how customers will benefit in the short term as well as long term. If reducing profits for one quarter or one year will give the company a boost over the competition for a decade because the new technology will take care of what matters, it is an easier decision to make.

Remember at all times that your job as a leader is to remind your people, at every opportunity, why what they do makes a difference, a difference that people care about, a difference that matters. Don't confuse a mission statement framed on the wall that clearly states what the company stands for with a grand mission that makes a difference to people. What you say and do every day in the halls of your business are a far more potent statement about what really matters in the business than anything printed anywhere (or everywhere) in your company.

Remind your people at every opportunity why what they do makes a difference.

- ## Participate in Intentional Leadership Discussions

Recall that this process starts with a clear statement of why a particular behavior makes a difference in the real mission of the business. This is no accident. Talk about everything in your business in terms of what really matters.

People will work hard and long hours for money. Often they will work pretty hard to satisfy a boss they like. Remember, though, that people will fight to the death for a grand mission. Find the grand mission in your business and tie what people do to that grand mission every chance you get.

There is a large hospital in the Midwest where the head of the facility has done an amazing job of reinforcing what really matters. You might think that hospitals have it easy when it comes to thinking about what really matters (after all, they are saving lives), but there are many hospitals out there with employees who are distracted from what matters on a regular basis by bad regulations, poor focus and long hours of work.

What you do every day is a much stronger statement of your mission than what is framed on the wall or in your annual report.

You can walk the halls of this hospital and ask any employee what they do, and somewhere in their explanation, without fail, will be a connection to the health, safety and longevity of patients. Clinical staff will tell you their jobs exist to provide comfort and aid to the sick and dying. Food preparation employees will tell you they pay attention to what food their patients eat, because it helps them regain their strength and health. Janitorial employees will say they reduce the chances of the spreading of disease and maintain a sanitary atmosphere for healing to occur. Administrative employees will tell you they provide the foundation for the work to be done with minimum distraction. This is more than a mission on a wall. These employees know every day that what they do is important. It matters.

- ## Start Every Meeting with What is Most Important

Structure your meeting agendas so the *first* item is about the heart of the business. Talk about it in ways that help people learn what is hard about the business, what can be done to be their best, and how to help each other do so.

If your company's grand mission is to have the most elegant technology in a particular market segment, starting off your meetings with a review of financial statements sends a contradictory message. You are undermining your own business.

What you talk about *first* matters. If your grand vision and mission for your company matter, put them first, repeatedly.

The heart of your company resides in your heart and soul, your spirit for making the most of this life you are living. Great leadership recognizes this daily.

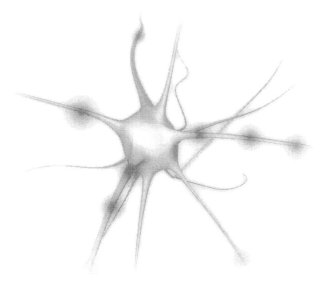

14.
Moving Forward

Nothing is impossible for the person who
doesn't have to do it.
--Unknown

With this book, we have offered you ways to think differently about how to interact effectively with others as well as how to manage your own side of that interaction. We have offered ways to behave that can help you generate a better, more effective balance between your old and new brains in the context of your business or organization. We have told you stories to help you view these suggestions in "real-world" terms, and we have explained at least in part why thinking and behaving differently gets you what you want.

One thing we have not done is tell you it is easy. In fact, we have worked to convey just the opposite understanding: that the level of personal challenge required to be and do your best as a leader does not reside in a list of recallable actions or a "cheat sheet," but rather requires real, sustainable change for most of us. The truth is that if the challenges we have presented in this book were easy, everyone would already be a great leader and we would have wasted our time writing this book!

As we have pointed out, our old brains can fool us into thinking it should be easy. You now know to be cautious of that kind of story. If it begins to feel easy, it is time to challenge your current story. You have been there before. There is an old adage that applies here: "if you always do what you've always done, you'll always get what you always got." You may become more comfortable with practice as you try new ways to help yourself and those around you do and be their best.

If you always do what you've always done, you'll always get what you always got.

But, beware the feeling of ease. The "Easy Button" made popular in ads for a U.S. office supplies store is a great marketing gimmick but it is not available as the path to effective leadership. That path entails turning your new brain for business loose on a regular basis.

Recall, if you will, the three rules of change that we presented previously: Change is slow; it is incremental; and it is painful. If one of these is missing, you might be fooling yourself about real change.

Because of this, we recommend an important goal in moving forward: intentionally commit each day to the small behavioral changes that over time become habits of great leadership. Avoid the challenge of transforming yourself. Instead, view the development of great leadership as an incremental process that will take some time. Beware the siren call of the quick fix, the "four pillars," the "21 irrefutable laws," or any of the other hundreds, if not thousands, of magical, mystical paths to great leadership. These are all music to your old brain. They sing, "Yes, you can have it all, right now, with no pain."

The more frequently you shape your intentions to use your new brain for business, the better your progress will be on your path to great leadership. To put it as plainly as possible, your clear intention each day for personal development is a necessary first step.

Intentionally commit each day to the small behavioral changes that, over time, become habits of great leadership.

Intentions do not make any difference until you turn them into behavior. The intentions might allow your old brain to feel like something has been accomplished, but accomplishment resides in action. So, your next step is to link your intentions to specific, intentional behavior. Many excellent suggestions are contained in this book, but this is not an exhaustive list. Try your own behavioral ideas as they occur to you, and then pay attention to what happens as a result. From reading this book, you now know to be on the lookout for signals of old brain activity, such as:

- overly simple solutions to complex problems where your language may include the phrase "if we would just...;"

- polarized language and First Best Answers;

- imperative language such as "should," "have to," and "must;"

- profanity;

- "me" or "I" language when you are wanting things to be different;
- focusing on the past.

If you find that your behaviors are producing these or many other kinds of responses, challenge your own story about what you are doing and look for alternatives to get to your desired goals.

As you begin to feel that your clear intentions and resulting behaviors are getting you some traction, test the reality of your beliefs. Perhaps you started out believing that people must be told what they have done wrong before they can understand how they can do something differently. Then, you decide that you will clearly intend to focus on the future, and tell people what you want, not what you do not like. You actually try this several times with someone and find, let's say, that that person's performance is beginning to improve. So, test your belief - do you still think people must be told what they have done wrong? This is a simple example, but you get the idea. As you rethink your beliefs, your intentions and resulting behaviors become more habitual and helpful to you and others.

Keeping the change you are undertaking small is a good idea. If you list all the suggestions in this book and make a commitment to do half of them tomorrow, and all of them by the end of the month, your chances for success are very, very low. Real change is incremental. Take the small steps every day - choose one new behavior and try it until you are comfortable with what you have done, then choose another. Relying on change via big leaps once in a while is a recipe for failure.

Because we know our old brains resonate with the "I Want It All" message, let's say this again. If it were easy, everyone, including you, would already be doing it. With so much of our daily lives (90-95%) driven by automatic, habitual behavior, change demands that we engage in the struggle of altering our habits. As anyone who has tried to lose weight, stop smoking, stop biting their fingernails, stop twirling their hair, or stop saying "you know" repeatedly can attest, change is hard work.

Becoming a great leader requires a commitment to do this hard work, in small chunks, every day. Treasure the awkward, stumbling feeling that comes with trying something new. It means you have overcome your old brain's drive to "make it easy."

Consider this: most people don't "feel" change happening. We usually see it looking back. In the moment, we feel the discomfort with newness and generate old brain stories that can help us stop the change process. Once we have moved past the hurdle of this discomfort, we can relax a bit and take that "third eye" look at ourselves and see the progress we have made. Another way to think about this is that when you have undertaken a change, it will make you uncomfortable and it may make others uncomfortable. Celebrating the discomfort instead of running from it or fighting it is a key part of the change process.

Great leadership is all about you, your intentions, but most importantly about your behavior. If your focus is on what others are doing and saying, assume that you are off target. If your stories about your own leadership entail the emotions, choices, and actions of others, you are falling into the trap of storytelling that makes you comfortable with your own emotions rather than on creating a story that leads to your being your best and helping others do the same.

Where you are right now as a leader (and as a person) is "normal." That is, you are where you should be, given your experiences to date. Like everyone else in the world, you have adapted to your circumstances, over time, to be who you are. Things that you do now were learned to serve you, in some way, in the past. The focus now is to ensure these things are serving you in the present.

Be kind to yourself.

Here is another key: be kind to yourself. Resist the old brain temptation to judge yourself harshly or critically. Be intentional in your internal behavior (thinking) as well as external behavior (action). Take responsibility for yourself, your thinking and your actions. Commit to engaging in behaviors that bring better balance between your old and new brain.

Unleashing the power of your new brain may seem like an easy task given that we use our new brain so much, especially with language. You know now, though, that our new brain is often usurped by our old brain's strong desire to keep us safe, leading to suboptimal outcomes, in life as well as business. This is a tough journey to make alone. Asking for help from others can make a critical difference.

As we have mentioned previously, your old brain can trick you and provide you with stories that keep you from being and doing your best. Often, others can see this in action long before we can see it ourselves. You will be rewarded if you find someone you trust enough to help you with this; someone who can, and is willing to, point out to you your old brain intrusions. This person can also provide you with some "benchmarking" to help you see the slow, incremental progress you are making. A trusted advisor or friend can point out to you when you are clinging to a story that is getting in the way of what you really want.

Choose this advisor carefully. It is no easy task to point out to others that their old brain is humming. Often it is akin to poking a stick into a beehive. It is helpful if your advisor is already adept at managing his or her own old brain eruptions, and can spare you from them in key moments.

Again, be kind to yourself. The 10:1 Rule isn't just for others. We shape our feelings in part by the language we use with ourselves, in our heads and out loud. Your old brain tendency to focus on what is wrong gets applied to you, too. Most of the behavioral suggestions we provide in this book work very well when applied to yourself. After all, if you can't do it for yourself, how do you imagine you will be at your best and do for others?

Our challenge to you is to be and do your best. Unleash your new brain for business.

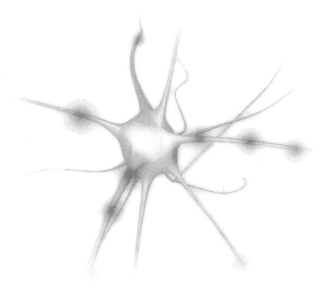

Acknowledgements

"Red" Smith, a famous sports writer, once commented that "There's nothing to writing. All you have to do is sit down at a typewriter and open a vein."

We're no longer laughing at that flippy little comment. Writing this book has involved years of pondering, discussing, feeling stumped, asking for help from others, and plodding away at the keyboard. It has also been one of the most fun and exciting activities either of us has taken on.

We have some people to thank for that. First and foremost, we want to express our heartfelt gratitude to Tim Bradley of Bradley Consulting Group in Denver, Colorado. A valued client for many years, Tim made up his mind that we should write this book and opened the first door to actually making it happen by offering up his place in the mountains to get it started. We spent a week there and did, in fact, get the writing of the book started in a big way.

Specifically, there are some people who got involved in the actual production of the book without whom the book would still be a set of files on our network. Our appreciation goes to Arienne McCracken for not pulling any punches in her editing and making excellent suggestions that added value to content and flow. Kirk Diedrich at Lucky Penny Productions worked closely with us on all the graphical design work and is a creative force in himself. Thank you, Kirk, for your hard work and incredible help.

Also a special thank you to cartoonists Marty Bucella, Ted Goff, and Sidney Harris for allowing us to use some of their brilliant illustrations of important concepts in this book.

Along the way, so many of our clients have challenged us to think about what really makes a difference, and to stay a step ahead in order to have value to offer. To all of you, we say thank you, because this book has resulted from your trust in us.

A client once asked us, "how much time did you spend preparing for this meeting," and we answered "about 25 years." This book is the result and we hope it is helpful in some way to every reader.

Rich Trafton and Diane Marentette

One more note: Much of what is in this book is built on my background in psychology. My education as a psychologist would have been less robust without my son, Alex. Participating in his development has provided more true understanding of human behavior and how it works than anything else in my life. I thank him for putting up with a psychologist for a father.

Rich Trafton

Quotes

Quotations that are separated from the text are captured below, with page numbers.

Quotes by Rich Trafton and Diane Marentette:

Personal change is slow, incremental and painful. If it is not all three, you are fooling yourself into thinking you are changing.   12

A key evolutionary lesson: Missed opportunity is much less costly than missed threat.   14

All perceptual information gets filtered by your old brain before anything else happens.   17

Our emotions often intrude on our thinking, but our thinking rarely intrudes on our emotions.   19

Our new brain analyzes. Our old brain chooses.   30

Great leaders first manage themselves, then help others bring their best to the table.   31

Negative reinforcement is NOT punishment!!   41

Quotes by Others:

*Be kind, for everyone you meet is fighting a hard
battle.*
--Plato   75

*Talent is always conscious of its own abundance, and
does not object to sharing.*
--Alexander Solzhenitsyn   111

*People don't care how much you know until they know
how much you care.*
-- Unknown   124

*All progress is precarious, and the solution of one
problem brings us face to face with another problem.*
--Martin Luther King, Jr.   132

Forgiveness is letting go of all hope for a better past.
--Unknown   151

*From the deepest desires often comes the deadliest
hate.*
--Socrates   172

Beware the barrenness of a busy life.
--Socrates   174

*Nothing is impossible for the person who doesn't have
to do it.*
--Unknown   179

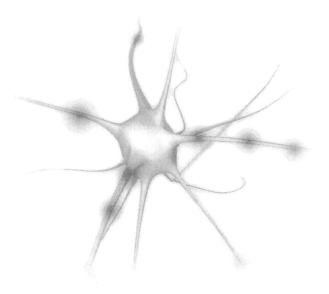

Index

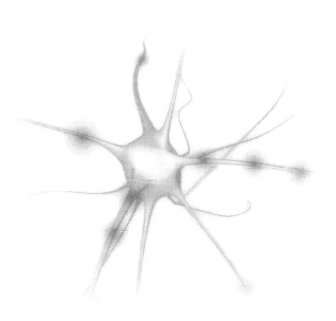